Managing Projects

Managing Projects serves as a comprehensive guide to the practice of project management, offering insights and methodologies useful to both novices and seasoned practitioners.

Each chapter is dedicated to a key component of project management, taking the reader through each stage involved in successful project delivery, from project initiation and planning to execution and closure. It also delves into the history of project management, acknowledging how the field has adapted to modern methods of working and the impact of this evolution on contemporary practices.

The book aims to

- Provide a clear and comprehensive understanding of project management principles, especially for those new to the field.
- Examine various project management methodologies, including both traditional and modern approaches, to give readers a broad perspective.
- Offer case studies and practical examples to demonstrate the application of project management principles in various scenarios.
- Emphasise the importance of balancing technical skills with the socio-cultural dynamics and leadership that influence project success.

Suitable for professionals as well as postgraduate and executive education students, *Managing Projects* serves as an invaluable resource for anyone looking to deepen their knowledge in the field of project management.

Alec Waterworth is an associate professor of project management at Montpellier Business School, France.

Carl Gavin is a professor of project management at Alliance Manchester Business School, University of Manchester, UK.

Management Practice Essentials

This series of Shortform textbooks has been developed to align with and support the Level 7 Senior Leader Master's Degree Apprenticeship (SLMDA). Each book concentrates on a key element of the SLMDA Standard and therefore covers a core essential of management practice. The series is centred around critical reflection on the underlying assumptions the individual leader or manager might make and their current practice, and collectively designed to enhance leadership knowledge, skills and behaviours. An ideal approach for any executive education course delivered through blended learning, and a useful alternative or supplement to traditional textbooks for a range of postgraduate Business & Management modules, the books:

- Combine theory and practice – providing students with knowledge and critical understanding of the theories, concepts and principles of leading organisations and focusing on the practical application and execution of these concepts;
- Are experience-led – providing students with the opportunity to develop their intellectual, practical and transferable skills and behaviours necessary to successfully analyse, develop and manage organisations.
- Include features to aid learning and understanding, such as chapter objectives, summaries, reflective questions and additional PowerPoint slides and cases available online.

Innovation and Entrepreneurship
Mike Kennard

Managing Projects
Alec Waterworth and Carl Gavin

For more information about the series, please visit www.routledge.com/Management-Practice-Essentials/book-series/MPE

Managing Projects

**Alec Waterworth and
Carl Gavin**

Routledge
Taylor & Francis Group

LONDON AND NEW YORK

First published 2024
by Routledge
4 Park Square, Milton Park, Abingdon, Oxon OX14 4RN

and by Routledge
605 Third Avenue, New York, NY 10158

Routledge is an imprint of the Taylor & Francis Group, an informa business

British Library Cataloguing-in-Publication Data
A catalogue record for this book is available from the British Library

ISBN: 9780367522681 (hbk)
ISBN: 9780367522711 (pbk)
ISBN: 9781003057246 (ebk)

DOI: 10.4324/9781003057246

Typeset in Times New Roman
by Newgen Publishing UK

Contents

Figures

About the Authors

Alec Waterworth is an associate professor of project management at Montpellier Business School. His teaching is focused on addressing complex organisational challenges across a wide range of sectors and contexts. In recent years, he has delivered project management and leadership development training to a wide range of organisations, including BAE Systems, BP, the UK Department of International Trade, the UK National Health Service, Arriva and Northern Trains. Previously, Alec was a lecturer within executive education at Alliance Manchester Business School and a senior teaching fellow at the University of Warwick. He has also worked as a Research Fellow at Warwick Business School, working closely with the UK Energy Research Centre. Before entering academia, Alec worked in the oil and gas industry as a Quality Assurance Engineer on several multi-billion US$ projects. Alec can be contacted via LinkedIn.

Carl Gavin is a professor of project management at Alliance Manchester Business School, University of Manchester, and is director of several bespoke executive education programmes—on project management, project leadership and project sponsorship—for multi-national companies delivering complex projects, including AWE, BAE Systems, BP, Cummins, National Trust, and Syngenta. Carl has 35 years' experience in project management, directing and managing large-scale projects for a diverse range of businesses and public-sector organisations, and prior to joining the University of Manchester, he was managing director of a projects-based business in the Northwest of England. Over the years, Carl has been chair of trustees of a number of public-sector organisations and social inclusion charities.

1 Introduction to Project Management

Introduction

Welcome to *Managing Projects*. Whether you are new to project work or you have been managing projects for years, you will find this book to be a highly valuable resource. In this first chapter, we will examine what is a 'project' and how does project work differ from ongoing work or business operations. Further, we outline the core components of effective project management, in addition to briefly discussing its historical development into the sophisticated management practice it is today. We examine project performance and the several lenses through which success can be measured on projects. Finally, we outline a typical project lifecycle—the *Waterfall* approach—which also provides the framework for the forthcoming chapters of the book, whilst also discussing the alternative project management approaches that exist, including *Agile* project management.

What Is a Project?

To start at the very beginning, what is a project? According to the Project Management Institute (PMI), a project is "a temporary endeavour undertaken to create a unique product, service, or result" (PMI, 2021). The Association of Project Management's (APM) definition of a project is similar: "a unique, transient endeavour undertaken to bring about change and to achieve planned objectives" (APM, 2019).

DOI: 10.4324/9781003057246-1

Projects are a temporary organisation of people, resources and processes delivering beneficial change for an organisation—be it new products and services, or new knowledge, assets, processes, and systems—to help meet the organisation's strategic need in responding to either the opportunities or threats of its environment. Work is planned and then undertaken to produce 'deliverables', which will in turn contribute towards the achievement of the strategy.

Projects are temporary in that they have a definite beginning and end, and the end of the project is reached when the project's planned objectives have been achieved (or will not/cannot be met), or when the project is otherwise terminated. A project is considered successful when it meets its objectives, typically within the agreed timeframe and budget. Therefore, a considerable focus of project work is directed at ensuring the project is completed within such a constrained environment: by a specific point in time and with similarly finite financial resources.

People have been undertaking projects for thousands of years, since the earliest days of organised human activity. Whether it be the construction of the pyramids of Giza or Heathrow Airport's Terminal 5, projects have been a way for people and organisations to drive change: to move from a current state to a desirable future state. Projects equally create value for a business, either tangible in the form of new assets, new processes, or increased market share, intangible in the form of brand recognition, strategic alignment, or enhanced reputation (PMI, 2021), or to support its survival and competitiveness in the future.

These characteristics of a project distinguish it from ongoing work or business operations. In contrast to projects, operations (i.e. 'business as usual') are repetitive and without an end date but are no less important, given their role in maintaining current business activities. Organisations must balance these two competing imperatives, with projects affecting operations over time, as the deliverables from projects become part of the day-to-day business operations.

Project Management

Project Management is the process by which we plan, organise, coordinate, lead, and control the activities and resources required to deliver the project and achieve its objectives:

- *Planning*, to outline what has to be done, how it will be done, and by whom, in a manner that is consistent with the organisation's goals for the project, the resources available, and the constraints under which the project must operate (e.g. time, budget, etc.; Nicholas and Steyn, 2008).
- *Organising,* in reference to the recruitment and training of project personnel, alongside organising these individuals into a hierarchy with clear lines of authority, responsibility, accountability, and decision-making; the acquisition of resources (i.e. facilities, machinery, materials, financial capital, etc.); and the underlying processes, procedures, policies, and lines of communication that will ensure the effective functioning of the project.
- *Coordinating* the work of every person and every organisation involved in the project is equally essential.
- *Leading* is crucial in directing the project and motivating project personnel and in securing the support of the project's wider stakeholders (e.g. customers, suppliers, regulators, corporate sponsors, etc.).
- Finally, *controlling,* by which we evaluate project performance and respond where necessary to address any deviation from the plan. Control also involves the management of change. Change is an inherent part of project work, as is *uncertainty:* projects are future-oriented, and the future is uncertain; and with this comes a need to effectively manage both planned and unplanned change over time (discussed further in Chapter 4).

As this description suggests, project management requires the integration of both socio-cultural (i.e. leadership, problem-solving, teamworking, negotiation, managing stakeholders, etc.) and technical management processes (e.g. scope management, scheduling, budgeting, reporting; Larson and Gray, 2018). Some project leaders can become preoccupied with making plans to the point where they neglect the softer skills of project work. Conversely, others will excel at the socio-cultural dimension, expending all their time on building strong team dynamics without making any concrete plans or organising the work taking place. Effective project management requires a balance of both the 'art' and the 'science' (this is reflected in the focus of this book).

As a practice, project management has come a long way in the last century. The early twentieth century saw the techniques used to manage construction projects adapted to non-construction jobs, such as designing and developing specialised machinery (Nicholas and Steyn, 2008). Soon thereafter, new planning approaches were deployed during the First World War, including the now-ubiquitous *Gantt chart* for the scheduling of activities (addressed further in Chapter 5).

By the mid-1950s, the term 'project management' had come into being (on the Atlas intercontinental ballistic missile project) and many of the established techniques for managing projects were being challenged by the increasing size and complexity of projects, as driven by rapid industrialisation, with projects increasingly suffering from huge cost and schedule overruns. More sophisticated approaches ensued, largely driven by large aerospace and defence projects, including *critical path analysis* for planning and scheduling (refer to Chapter 5) and *earned value* (refer to Chapter 7), and the adoption of computerised data processing to handle the vast volumes of information generated by such large-scale projects (Lock, 2013).

The 1970s saw rapid growth in the use of information technology and the introduction of specialised project management software, although this remained the domain of IT experts. The 1980s opened up project management software to a wider audience with the dawn of the desktop computer, and data processing times were cut dramatically. The late-1980s and 1990s saw a proliferation of best practice project management methods (such as PRINCE2) and 'bodies of knowledge', published by professional bodies and management consultancies.

The last thirty years has seen a greater focus on communication, with project managers aided further by increased computerisation and the Internet. Project management has become increasingly proactive: focusing on predicting risk events and planning contingencies and risk mitigation strategies (refer to Chapter 4; Lock, 2013). Many projects are now supported by real-time data processing, with up-to-the-minute data collected whilst the related task is still happening, allowing project personnel to view and report the status of tasks (and the project as a whole) at any given time, in the most current form possible.

The Project Manager

The Project Manager is the "person assigned by the performing organisation to lead the project team that is responsible for achieving the project objectives" (PMI, 2021). They are usually directly answerable for the project's schedule, budget, and results (Kloppenborg, 2009). They are typically involved in the project throughout its lifecycle, from initiation to planning to execution and close. This is, in fact, one of the key distinctions that can be drawn between project managers and functional managers: functional managers take over existing operations, whereas project managers create a project team and organisation that did not exist before and have a significant say in how the project will be managed, rather than simply following predefined processes.

The Project Manager is the person ultimately responsible for project performance and managing the trade-offs that are made between the customer expectations, the constraints the project must operate under, and what is viable and achievable. At the same time, unlike functional managers, project managers typically do not possess the technical knowledge to make such decisions alone and thus must ensure the right people, at the right time, make the right decisions (Larson and Gray, 2018). They must be able to motivate individuals, creating a vision of success and offering clear direction in support of this. They may also contribute towards advancing the project management competency and capability within the wider organisation (PMI, 2021).

Above all else, it is a role for an effective communicator—they are an integrator for the project: leading the various project sub-teams and liaising with a diverse range of stakeholders, whilst also coordinating with the organisation's functional groups (Merrow and Nandurdikar, 2018). This integration role extends to strategy, and it is the responsibility of the Project Manager to review the objectives of the wider organisation and ensure an alignment with those of the project and the work being performed. This requires effective and consistent communication with those charged with oversight over the project (discussed in Chapter 2).

We will continue to define the role of the Project Manager throughout our exploration of project management in the remainder of the book. For now, we turn our attention to project performance.

Project Performance

A successful project is one that creates deliverables that meet the prescribed requirements of the owner, customer, or end user. Whilst 'quality management' is an important practice on projects, a broader conceptualisation of *quality* on projects is simply "the degree to which a set of inherent characteristics fulfils requirements" (PMI, 2021). The requirements will be developed into a scope of work, described as "the sum of all products, services and results to be provided by the project" (ibid.). We discuss gathering of requirements in Chapter 3 and the development of a scope of work in Chapter 4.

The scope of work, and the underpinning requirements, must be balanced against a set of constraints. As discussed, almost all

Figure 1.1 The Project Management Triangle.

projects will, at the very least, have time and cost constraints (i.e. very few projects have a bottomless budget, nor an indefinite timescale). This relationship between scope, cost, and time, and its impact on quality on a project, can be illustrated as shown in Figure 1.1. The 'project management triangle' (also known as the 'iron triangle' or 'triple constraint') of cost, time, and scope was developed by Martin Barnes at the University of Manchester in the early 1970s to argue that making a change to one of the constraints affects the other two.

Ensuring the scope and desired quality is achieved on a project under constraints of time and cost presents a significant challenge. For this reason, plans are put in place, such as budgets and schedules, to ensure that these requirements and constraints are considered and planned for systematically. However, there are many things that can derail a project from its planned course, and, similarly, opportunities may arise to exceed the original expectations. There is a delicate balance between not just the requirements and the constraints but between the constraints themselves (i.e. were we to change the project scope to add additional features to a product, this would certainly challenge our ability to deliver on time and on budget; reducing the schedule by three months will equally impair our ability to deliver the complete scope on budget). This requires continuous management throughout the project lifecycle. In addition, the prioritisation of these constraints will be different across different projects, and the perception of success and failure will differ accordingly. For some projects, the budget absolutely cannot be exceeded but the schedule can flex, whereas on others, the project must be delivered on time, even if it means the scope is not entirely fulfilled. Effective project management also requires us to alter our approach to suit the nature of the project in this regard.

Success can also be measured in terms of the benefits to the parent organisation. Projects are an excellent source of organisational learning, and a successful project will lead to new skills, competencies, technologies, and efficiencies. These insights from projects should be captured and shared within the wider parent organisation, as we discuss in Chapter 8. A successful project will also deliver further business results to the parent organisation, such as the development of further new products and/or services, an increased market share, a stronger reputation, or increased profitability.

The Project Lifecycle

The project lifecycle describes the series of stages that a project passes through from the first day of the project through to its closure. The stages can be sequential, iterative, or overlapping.

Project lifecycles exist on a continuum from predictive to adaptive. Predictive lifecycles (also termed *linear* or *Waterfall*) are better suited to projects with a high degree of certainty: the project scope, timescale, and cost can be determined in the early stages of the lifecycle, and any changes to the scope can be diligently managed thereafter against that baseline. Adaptive lifecycles (also referred to as *Agile* or *evolutionary*), where

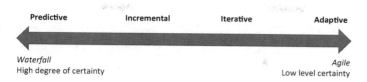

Figure 1.2 Project Lifecycle Continuum.

it is accepted that planning and unpredictable change occurs throughout the project lifecycle, are most appropriate to projects with low levels of certainty. This is illustrated in Figure 1.2.

There are a further two types of lifecycle:

- In an *incremental* lifecycle, the deliverable is produced through a staged series of smaller increments, which successively add functionality within a predetermined timeframe (PMI, 2021). The deliverable will only be considered complete upon fulfilment of the final iteration. Such an approach can be used to deliver 'quick wins', conserve resources where scarce, or deliver early benefits to the customer (APM, 2019).
- In an *iterative* lifecycle, the project scope is determined early on, but time and cost estimates are routinely adjusted as the project team's understanding of the requirements for the desired deliverable increases (PMI, 2021). The deliverable evolves through a series of repeated cycles. The use of prototyping can prove effective here, and such an approach also allows feedback for unfinished work to be collected so as to improve the final deliverable.

Further to this is the notion of *hybrid* lifecycles, whereby a combination of predictive and adaptive lifecycle stages is used. Those elements around which there is a high degree of certainty follow a predictive lifecycle, whereas those that are still uncertain follow an adaptive lifecycle to allow for a higher degree of change over time.

This is certainly not the case of one lifecycle approach being better than any other. Rather, project professionals must select the most appropriate for their project context.

Given that *Waterfall* and *Agile* are the two dominant approaches, we will examine each in further detail here.

Waterfall

In a *Waterfall* approach, project activities are sequenced into a collection of distinct stages, with each stage completed in turn, spanning the entirety of the project. All project work is completed through a single pass of the lifecycle. This division into stages is useful in supporting effective planning, as it provides a framework for drawing up budgets and schedules, allocating resources and project personnel, and defining milestones and review activities (APM, 2019). The stages are carried out in sequence, and each stage defines a set of activities and deliverables to be completed before proceeding to the next stage. As this description suggests, this is a highly structured approach, focused on predictability and stability, that lends itself to control, oversight, and governance. As previously discussed, it is assumed here that there is a high level of certainty and a comprehensive understanding of the project context, with relatively little scope for unpredictable change. A graphical representation of a typical *Waterfall* lifecycle is shown in Figure 1.3.

Here, we have based the names of each stage in the lifecycle on the terminology used by the PMI (2023). You will find

Figure 1.3 Waterfall Project Lifecycle.

different terminology used across different organisations and research institutes: for example, the APM utilises *concept, definition, deployment,* and *transition* (APM, 2019). Similarly, whilst typically expressed as four stages, you will find representations of a project lifecycle that are three, five, six, or seven stages. Nevertheless, most lifecycles will align with the following distinct stages:

- *Initiating:* following the identification of a need or objective for the project (typically a problem or opportunity to be addressed), high-level requirements are gathered from the customer/end user, and an assessment of the project's viability is made. This is typically detailed in a *business case* and, if the project is selected, this is developed further into a *project charter.*
- *Planning:* building on the work from the *Initiating* stage, a detailed definition of the project and the justification for the work (the *what* and the *why*) are outlined in the form of plans and requirements listings. This will include defining the project scope and resource requirements, developing a schedule and budget, and identifying risks.
- *Execution:* the plans are put into action, along with a continuous process of verifying actual progress against what was planned. Corrective action is taken when necessary to bring progress back in line with the plan (or to adjust the plan, which remains a 'living' document).
- *Closing:* involves a diverse set of activities, including the release of the final deliverables to the customer, collecting and making final payments, archiving project documentation, evaluating the performance of project personnel, and recording lessons learned from the project experience.

We adopt this four-stage framework as the structure for the book, with Chapter 3 examining *Initiating*, Chapters 4 to 6 addressing *Planning*, and Chapters 7 and 8 discussing *Execution* and *Closing*, respectively.

Between each of the stages in the project lifecycle are 'stage gates' (which may be referred to by other terms, such as 'phase gates', 'phase reviews', and 'decision gates'). The purpose of these gates is to review the project's progress and performance before allowing the project to proceed to the subsequent stage. These gates can be:

- *Soft:* any identified rework is agreed to be undertaken in the subsequent stage but the project nevertheless moves forward and the previous stage closes;
- *Hard:* any rework must be completed within the earlier stage before the project can proceed;
- *Fuzzy*: any rework is completed within the earlier stage. The compliant work moves forward but the non-compliant work is reworked, with the earlier stage remaining open until completed.

We will discuss stage gates further in Chapter 2 in the context of project governance.

Agile

The *Agile* method is the absolute opposite to the *Waterfall* approach. Under such an adaptive approach, we know the start point and the end goal but the high levels of uncertainty require flexibility with regards to how to accomplish it. A broad plan will be developed in the early stages of the project, but this will evolve iteratively over time in response to testing and experimentation, adding more detail in response to a growing understanding of what the solution might look like and how to realise it. It may be the most appropriate method in exploratory contexts where the requirements and scope are expected to change over time and the new technology needs to be tested (such as software development, product development, innovation projects, or research).

As with a *Waterfall* approach, gathering an initial robust set of customer requirements is a crucial part of the early work on

Agile projects. Hereafter, the project is planned and executed in short increments, called 'sprints' (also known as 'timeboxes'), usually a maximum of four weeks in duration. The objective of each sprint is to develop a workable product that satisfies one or more of the desired product features, which can then be demonstrated to the customer (in this sense, it is both *incremental* and *iterative*). At the end of each sprint, the customer (and other stakeholders) reviews the progress that has been made, reassesses the project objectives and requirements, and determines the adjustments that are required. A new sprint then begins, which will subsume the preceding work and add new features to the evolving product (shown in Figure 1.4). The objective of each sprint is simply to add value towards the project's objectives. The project concludes in a similar fashion to *Waterfall* projects with a closing stage that involves the handover of deliverables to the customer and a post-project review. Decision gates are an important part of the process but are timebound (i.e. coming at the end of each sprint), rather than event driven, and offer a valuable opportunity to reflect on what has been learned from the preceding sprint and how this will inform the next one.

Some of the key differences between *Waterfall* and *Agile* project management are summarised in Figure 1.5.

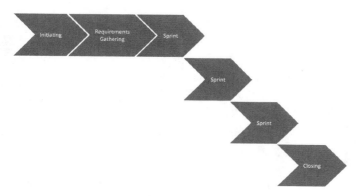

Figure 1.4 Agile Project Lifecycle.

Waterfall	Agile
Design up front	Continuous design
Fixed scope	Flexible scope
Freeze design as early as possible	Freeze design as late as possible
Low uncertainty	High uncertainty
Avoid change	Embrace change
Low customer interaction	High customer interaction
Conventional project teams	Self-organised teams

Figure 1.5 Waterfall vs. Agile Project Management (Adapted from Larson and Gray, 2018).

An increasing number of companies are embracing *Agile* methods as a way to reduce development time, foster innovation, and reduce risk (Kloppenborg, 2009). Projects can also benefit from greater customer involvement, whereby the customer can offer feedback on the deliverables to date and can further refine the requirements accordingly, also enhancing the likelihood that the end product will satisfy the customer. The key limitation to the approach is that it is incompatible with a need for scope, budget, and schedule control: at the project's outset, it is not clear how much it will cost, how long it will take, nor what the final product will look like.

As noted above, it is the responsibility of the project leadership to determine which approach is most appropriate for the project context.

Summary

This chapter has addressed the question "what is project management" and moreover "why does it matter?" Projects are an invaluable way of creating value for businesses, be it a new technology, product or service, a more efficient process, an increased market share, or an enhanced reputation. However, every project faces significant challenges along the way and must satisfy a set of requirements in a manner that also balances the constraints under which it must operate. The concept of 'quality' is a very important one for project work, in that it conveys this balance that must be struck and the complex and dynamic relationship between the various constraints. We have also examined the project lifecycle, which describes the distinct activities that must be performed during the life of the project. Whilst *Waterfall* is by far the most common, we have also drawn attention to the alternative approaches that exist, as well as the possibility to adopt a hybrid of these if deemed most suitable for a particular project.

We should emphasise that, whilst the book is structured in accordance with a typical *Waterfall* approach, the content of the book is generally applicable to the practice of project management irrespective of which approach is adopted.

The next chapter will examine the important role of governance on projects, before we then turn our attention to the four stages of the project lifecycle in turn.

References

APM (2019). *APM Body of Knowledge* (7th ed.), Princes Risborough: Association for Project Management.

Kloppenborg, T. (2009). *Project Management: A Contemporary Approach*, London: Cengage Learning.

Larson, E.W. and Gray, C.F. (2018). *Project Management: The Managerial Process* (7th ed.), New York: McGraw-Hill Education.

Lock, D. (2013). *Project Management* (10th ed.), London: Gower.

Merrow, E.W. and Nandurdikar, N. (2018). *Leading Complex Projects: A Data-Driven Approach to Mastering the Human Side of Project Management*, Oxford: Wiley.

Nicholas, J.M. and Steyn, H. (2008). *Project Management for Business, Engineering and Technology: Principles and Practice* (3rd ed.), Oxford: Butterworth-Heinemann.

PMI (2021). *A Guide to the Project Management Body of Knowledge (PMBOK Guide)* (7th ed.), Newtown Square, PA: Project Management Institute.

PMI (2023). *Process Groups: A Practice Guide*, Newtown Square, PA: Project Management Institute.

2 Project Selection and Governance

Introduction

In Chapter 1, we discussed the use of projects by organisations to develop new products, services, and processes. In this chapter, we will examine this further in considering how projects serve an organisation's strategy and the underpinning mechanisms that ensure projects remain aligned to its strategic objectives. This involves both *doing the right projects* and *doing those projects right*. As such, we will examine how organisations come to select and prioritise projects so as to maximise their collective contribution to achieving strategic objectives. We will also address the governance process that assures that a project is performing as planned, remains viable and achievable, and is following the organisation's established best practice for project management. Around this theme of governance, we also highlight the crucial role of those outside the project team: specifically, the Project Sponsor, the Steering Committee, and the Project Management Office.

Organisational Strategy and Projects

We will start by examining the relationship between an organisation's strategy and the projects in which it chooses to invest time and resources. Maylor and Turner (2022) discuss the 'traditional' and 'strategic' approaches to managing projects within a wider organisational context. In a traditional approach,

DOI: 10.4324/9781003057246-2

there is a weak link between the project's objectives and the organisational strategy and a lack of coordination between the organisation's various projects (leading to conflicts over resources). This is historically how projects were implemented, with a sole focus on the planning and execution of the project, rather than how it might benefit the strategic aims of the organisation (Larson and Gray, 2018). Today, project management is recognised as existing hand-in-hand with strategic management, and thus a strategic approach focuses on establishing a strong, bi-directional link between the organisational strategy and the organisation's projects. Projects emerge from the strategic decisions taken, and equally project experience will inform organisational strategy over time. Given the complex challenges that project-based organisations face today, the holistic, coordinated approach is the only choice for long-term, sustainable success.

Kloppenborg et al. (2019) outline the steps from strategic planning through to project selection. It starts with *strategic analysis*: an ongoing process by which the organisation analyses both the internal and external environments to determine where threats or opportunities may exist. The former might address the strengths and weaknesses of the organisation and its personnel; the latter will be focused more on its customers, end users, competitors, technologies, etc.

This detailed understanding of the internal and external environment can be translated into the vision and mission of the organisation. The vision outlines the long-term desirable change that the organisation is focused on bringing. It conveys a desirable future state: "what we want to become" (Larson and Gray, 2018). However, "it is something to be pursued, but not expected to ever end" (Wysocki, 2019).

The mission is how the vision will be carried out and should include the organisation's purpose, core values, culture, primary business areas, and primary customers/end users. The mission establishes a shared understanding with all the organisation's personnel and its stakeholders of these key facets of the organisation's identity.

With a vision and mission established, the setting of strategic objectives is the next step in achieving these. These will typically be mid- to long-term objectives—often achievable in well over a year—and will form the basis of regular strategic planning activities for the organisation. They will address how internal weaknesses can be improved and strengths can be maximised; and how threats from the market and signals from customers can be translated into opportunities. The objectives should be conveyed in clear, specific, and measurable terms.

The strategic objectives will then provide a focus for decision-making regarding the selection and prioritisation of projects (addressed later in this chapter).

As this suggests, projects should be reflective of and aligned to the organisation's strategy. Jamieson and Morris (2004) offer a useful framework for how to translate organisational strategy into project strategy, which incorporates guidance from both the PMI's and APM's 'Body of Knowledge' Guides (the *PMBOK* and *APMBOK*, respectively; PMI, 2021, 2023; APM, 2019). The process starts with project definition, in which the vision for the project is outlined, the purpose of the project is defined, the project plans are aligned with those of the parent organisation, and the basis of cooperation for the project is agreed upon (refer to Chapter 3). Thereafter, this can be developed into a scope of work—as described in Chapter 4—which starts with aligning the project with the ongoing work of the organisation (i.e. a particular market demand or business need that, it is hoped, the project will satisfy). As such, the business strategy of the parent organisation remains an important input here in both guiding project selection decisions and in developing a project strategy that is aligned to that of the wider organisation. There is ample evidence that this is a weak point for many organisations (Larson and Gray, 2018).

Many organisations utilise a hierarchy of projects, organised into programmes (i.e. collections of projects) and portfolios (i.e. collections of programmes and projects). The management of these as a hierarchy of nested projects, programmes and portfolios—managed in an integrated and coordinated manner—can be used as a means of implementing business strategy throughout a diverse array of projects, thus increasing their collective potential to further the organisation's competitive advantage. This is where we now turn our attention.

Projects, Programmes, and Portfolios

Projects can be managed under three distinct arrangements (PMI, 2021): (i) as a stand-alone project; (ii) within a programme; or (iii) within a portfolio. We can view this as a hierarchy, with an organisation operating one or more portfolios, within which are programmes comprised of a collection of projects, as well as, possibly, some stand-alone projects, where:

- A *Project* is a set of activities managed in a systemic way to achieve a desired output (e.g. product, service, business change). It may be standalone or part of a programme.
- A *Programme* is a collection of related projects that, when integrated together, result in a desired outcome (e.g. objective, goal, benefit). It may be part of a portfolio. Programmes are typically responsible for organic growth and (sometimes) new business within an organisation.
- A *Portfolio* is a collection of unrelated (or loosely related) projects, programmes and/or operations that are coordinated to achieve strategic objectives. This requires a balance of maintaining business as usual, maximising return on investment, and the implementation of change initiatives (APM, 2019). A portfolio is sometimes referred to as a 'business unit' (or depending on the organisation, could be within a business unit with a number of portfolios).

It is important to emphasise here the different strategic purpose that each of these serves the wider organisation. This is reflected in how each must be managed and led. The programme management process has the same structure as the project management process described in the preceding chapter (i.e. planning, organising, coordinating, controlling and leading). However, a programme is typically longer-term than the projects that comprise it: some of the projects will be performed sequentially whilst some will be performed in parallel. Whereas project leadership is focused entirely on the delivery of current commitments, programme leadership must balance current commitments with safeguarding the programme's health and ensuring its future phases will not face shortfalls in resources. Planning is benefits-led, focusing on what to do next to effectively deliver outcomes and benefits, rather than what to do to deliver outputs or products (APM, 2019).

The methodologies used in programme management are also similar to those used in project management (which will be outlined in the subsequent chapters of this book), such as breakdown structures, schedules, and risk analysis. However, if programme leaders adopt a performance-only mindset (as per project work), the benefits are lost. Rather, programmes exist to create benefits that exceed those that an individual project can generate on its own (Thiry, 2004) and must be led as such. Programme managers must endeavour to remain focused on the planning and control of the programme, rather than getting into the weeds of individual projects. However, there will be opportunities to support project managers in addressing high-level issues (i.e. adopting the role of 'Project Sponsor', which we will come to later in this chapter). They will be supported by their programme team members and programme office, who collectively strive to ensure the integration of the different projects within the programme so as to fulfil the programme's objectives/goals.

Portfolio leaders must remain focused on setting strategic direction and securing future business for the organisation, balanced with the portfolio's current commitments. Whereas programme and project management is about *doing the programmes and projects right*, portfolio management is about *doing the right programmes and projects* (Jamieson and Morris, 2004), with projects and programmes selected and prioritised based on their ability to deliver the organisation's strategic objectives. This also requires balancing resource demand with resource availability. At this level, the shared activities and methods between project and programme management are significantly less evident, and there is a much greater focus on business strategy and company-wide integration. In managing a portfolio, problems are centred less around managing individual projects and instead on issues related to resource allocation, politics, sponsorship and governance, and culture, as is the nature of overseeing a global, overlapping, and interdependent set of projects (Archer and Ghasemzadeh, 2004). There are several critical and dynamic factors that must be carefully balanced here, such as: the relative priority of corporate goals; quantitative and qualitative benefits; short-term vs. long-term gains; changing external requirements (e.g. regulatory, technological, political); availability of key resources and the allocation of people; and the risk profile of each project or programme in the portfolio (APM, 2019).

This highlights the challenge of selecting and then operating a diverse project portfolio whilst also ensuring that every project remains aligned to the organisation's strategic objectives (Wells and Kloppenborg, 2015). The remainder of this chapter will examine how an organisation can select the right projects, support their progress over time, and ensure their development remains aligned with the organisation's established approach to project management (i.e. doing the right projects and then doing those projects right).

Project Selection and Prioritisation

Every organisation must make choices around which projects it will invest in: resources are scarce, and organisations are generally not in a position to invest in every project. Logically, organisations must select and prioritise those projects that contribute the most to its objectives. Kloppenborg (2009) offers some guiding questions for the project selection process (whereby a potential project is selected or not to proceed to the planning stage):

* What value does the potential project bring to the organisation?
* Are the demands of performing the project well understood?
* Are the resources needed to perform the project available?
* Is there enthusiastic support for the project from both external customers and one (or more) internal champions?
* Are there rival projects that might better help the organisation achieve its goals?

This can be a complicated decision-making process, as each project will differ with regards to its resource requirements, risk exposure, cost, and strategic value. At least part of the process will be based around a financial assessment of the potential project (various approaches for which are outlined in Chapter 3). In addition, non-financial factors are typically also included, which, along with the financial assessment, can form the basis for a 'scoring model' for selecting projects, in the first instance, and thereafter in their prioritisation.

A scoring model is a simple tool for evaluating projects based on a set of criteria. The first step of establishing a scoring model is to identify the criteria that will be used. These should be linked to the organisation's strategic objectives, along with considerations such as risk, timescale, cost, etc. The criteria can then be weighted according to their relative importance. This can be done in one of three ways: (i) rated on a scale (for example 1–5), with the higher the number indicating the higher its priority; (ii) rank ordered, so that if there are four criteria, each is given a number from 1 to 4 depending on whether it is the first, second, third, or least important, with the most important scored 4 and the least important scored 1; and (iii) the Pugh method, whereby a baseline is established (i.e. criteria x is the most important) and given the maximum score, with

Project	Risk Level 3		Cost 2		Return on Investment 5		Value to Customer 4		Total Weighted Score
Project A	5		3		3		2		
		15		6		15		8	**44**
Project B	3		4		2		3		
		9		8		10		12	**39**
Project C	2		3		2		3		
		6		6		10		12	**34**
Project D	1		3		4		5		
		3		6		20		20	**49**

Figure 2.1 Example Project Selection and Prioritisation Model.

the other criteria then scored against that baseline. The example shown in Figure 2.1 uses the 'rated on a scale' approach.

Each project option can now be evaluated against each criterion. Quantitative data should be used wherever possible to make these assessments, and having the input of experienced project personnel can also be very valuable. The upper left-portion of each cell in the model can be used to display the assessed score, representing how well that project satisfies the criterion. It is easiest here to use the same scoring scale as the criteria ranking. It is also best to assess the various project options against a single criterion before moving on to the next criterion. The score for a project against a criterion is multiplied by the criterion weighting, which gives a weighted score. These are then tallied to provide a total weighted score for each of the project options. If several projects have identical or close scores, there is the option to introduce additional criteria to

Project	Risk Level 3		Cost 4		Return on Investment 5		Value to Customer 2		Total Weighted Score
Project A	5		3		3		2		
		15		12		15		4	**46**
Project B	3		4		2		3		
		9		16		10		6	**41**
Project C	2		3		2		3		
		6		12		10		6	**34**
Project D	1		3		4		5		
		3		12		20		10	**45**

Figure 2.2 Revised Example Project Selection and Prioritisation Model.

the model or to simply have a discussion, by way of breaking the tie.

Scoring models also allow decision-makers to perform 'sensitivity analyses': a way of examining how a change in circumstances might impact the criteria selected, how these are prioritised, and/or how the project options are scored against these criteria. Taking the example from Figure 2.1, this company might decide that were they to have a poor financial year then the prioritisation of 'Cost' would increase to a rating of 4 and 'Value to customer' would decrease to 2 (see Figure 2.2). In this case, Project D would no longer be the highest-scored option.

The model can also be used as an input into the process of prioritising projects, which requires balancing the timing, funding, and resource requirements of both new and ongoing projects. As such, beyond the model itself, the decision-makers will also need to hold discussions around other issues, such as (Kloppenborg, 2009):

- The urgency of each project.
- The cost of delaying the expected benefits from various projects.
- The practical details concerning the timing of projects, and
- Any potential resource conflict between various projects.

A further consideration here is the need for balance in the portfolio. Many organisations avoid taking on too much risk, choosing rather to diversify their portfolio in finding a balance between projects that are high-risk, high-gain, with those that are low-risk but low-gain (Nicholas and Steyn, 2008). Beyond risk, there are further considerations such as resource demand, cost, duration, and type (e.g. revenue generating vs. non-revenue generating). This is an additional assessment to the one already discussed and requires a perspective over the entire organisation and its project portfolio. It may be necessary to delay or reject a project that is evaluated through a scoring model (or similar process) to be very valuable because the organisation already has too many projects within its portfolio with the same characteristics. Organisations must evaluate what each new project will contribute to the portfolio, in addition to the achievement of strategic objectives: short-term needs must be balanced with long-term potential, and resource allocation must be optimised across all projects, not just the highest-priority ones (Larson and Gray, 2018).

Even with careful planning and prioritisation of projects, the organisation's strategic objectives will change over time, new opportunities will arise, exposure to risk may increase (or the organisation's appetite for risk may change), and resources might become unexpectedly constrained. As such, this prioritisation process should be an ongoing evaluation for organisations, which sees some projects accelerated and others delayed or cancelled in response to changing conditions.

Similarly, if a project is assessed to not be meeting its expected benefits or operating within its agreed constraints, this may also lead to its delay or cancellation. This assessment falls under the project management process of governance (i.e. doing projects right), to which we now turn our attention.

Project Governance

Once a project has been selected, there is an ongoing need for governance. Governance is the means by which organisations establish control over projects, programmes, and portfolios through a framework of rules and expectations that provide "the structure through which the objectives of the company are set, and the means of attaining those objectives and monitoring performance" (OECD, 2004). It dictates how organisations oversee the management of all their projects, how projects are selected, how they can ensure performance measurement and accountability, and how to continually improve project management in the whole organisation over time (Larson and Gray, 2018).

The APM offers the following 'Principles of Project Governance' (APM, 2011):

1 The board has overall responsibility for the governance of project management.
2 The organisation differentiates between project- and non-project-based activities.
3 Roles and responsibilities for the governance of project management are defined clearly.
4 Disciplined governance arrangements supported by appropriate cultures, methods, resources, and controls are applied throughout the project life cycle. Every project has a sponsor.
5 There is a demonstrable coherent and supporting relationship between the project portfolio and the business strategy and policies, for example ethics and sustainability.

6 All projects have an approved plan containing authorisation points at which the business case, inclusive of cost, benefits, and risk, is reviewed. Decisions made at authorisation points are recorded and communicated.

7 Members of delegated authorisation bodies have sufficient representation, competence, authority, and resources to enable them to make appropriate decisions.

8 Project business cases are supported by relevant and realistic information that provides a reliable basis for making authorisation decisions.

9 The board or its delegated agents decide when independent scrutiny of projects or project management systems is required and implement such assurance accordingly.

10 There are clearly defined criteria for reporting project status and for the escalation of risks and issues to the levels required by the organisation.

11 The organisation fosters a culture of improvement and of frank internal disclosure of project management information.

12 Project stakeholders are engaged at a level that is commensurate with their importance to the organisation and in a manner that fosters trust.

13 Projects are closed when they are no longer justified as part of the organisation's portfolio.

This demonstrates the reach of project governance: The first four are self-referential; principles 5 and 6 emphasise the need for strategic alignment between the organisation and its projects; 7 and 8 address the importance of people and information; 9 and 13 refer to governance; 10 to risk; 11 to organisational improvement; and 12 to stakeholders (as summarised by Morris, 2013). These are all themes that we address in this or later chapters.

An effective governance framework (and supporting processes) will clearly establish the roles of accountability and authority in the organisation's practice of defining and thereafter controlling projects, programmes, and portfolios. It involves both financial and technical control over project-based work, including monitoring project progress against budget and milestones; ensuring the business case remains viable; providing strategic direction on issues and changes; ensuring organisational standards, processes, and procedures are being properly applied; and facilitating the removal of organisational blockages to successful project completion (Powell and Young, 2004).

A key component to establishing a governance framework is the assignment of roles and responsibilities to the project team and the wider stakeholders, for which a RACI matrix (described in detail in Chapter 5) can prove effective. This should be established early in the project and maintained throughout the lifecycle.

There is no one governance framework that is effective for all organisations, and as such, it must be tailored to the organisation's culture, types of projects, and the needs of the organisation (PMI, 2021).

Whilst governance is applied throughout the lifecycle, it plays a particularly important role as part of the stage gate process (discussed in Chapter 1). Decision points are established at the stage gates of the lifecycle, at which time various checks are completed to ensure all the necessary work has been completed before the project can proceed to the subsequent stage. This process is conducted by the Project Sponsor or wider governance body (known under various titles, such as Steering Committee, Steering Group, or Project Board), which we discuss in the subsequent sub-section. The decision point will typically ask four questions (APM, 2019):

- What has been achieved?
- What is required for the next stage?
- What are the key decisions to be made?
- Is the business case still viable (i.e. can the desired benefits be achieved at an acceptable level of cost and risk)?

These decision points are also an excellent opportunity to open a dialogue between the project leadership and its stakeholders. Project leaders can seek assistance or guidance in resolving issues, reaffirm stakeholder support, and highlight recent achievements. Decision points must not be treated as mere formality, however, and the sponsor must remain objective in making the right decision for the organisation. The project should not be allowed to continue if there is no longer a viable business case. This process is distinct from portfolio management: it does not consider any other projects or the impact of the project on organisational resources or strategic objectives, and the project is typically allowed to continue as long as it has met a set of pre-agreed criteria. The use of decision points augments portfolio management but certainly does not lessen the importance of diligence in the latter.

Finally, reporting is a further important component of project governance. When working effectively, this will ensure that the sponsor and other stakeholders and senior leaders are kept informed of the project's progress and are provided with the necessary information required to make decisions about the future investment of the project (or programme or portfolio; APM, 2019).

Project Sponsor

Often described as a vital or critical role (e.g. Morris, 2013; APM, 2019), the Project Sponsor actually assumes several roles. The first is in providing oversight, as the person accountable for ensuring the work is governed effectively and delivers the anticipated outcomes and benefits. As such, it is very important that this crucial role is filled by an individual with the status and authority within the organisation to enable them to assert a significant influence over the deployment of the project and its stakeholders (APM, 2019). The sponsor is also a champion of the project, ensuring the project receives the necessary funding and resources. They will also provide enthusiasm, guidance, and assistance as required. As such, this requires them to establish supportive working relationships with the project team, motivating them during challenging times and supporting them in addressing issues (Gavin and Forsyth, 2021). Further, the sponsor helps to establish the culture of the project and its working practices (Morris, 2013).

Typically, the sponsor will not devote much time to the project—as the role is often in addition to their own day-to-day leadership responsibilities—but should nevertheless be involved and remain available to the Project Manager throughout the project lifecycle. Their role is particularly significant in the early and closing stages of the project: establishing the client's needs and project's requirements to develop a business case and secure funding in the first instance and to take responsibility for the effective closing of the project to its conclusion (APM, 2019) and for tracking the resulting benefits post-project close. In this regard, the role often both precedes and supersedes that of the Project Manager.

Steering Committee

Typically chaired by the Project Sponsor, the Steering Committee comprises representatives of the functions and departments of the organisation that will be affected by, or are investing in, the project. As with the sponsor, the duties of the Steering Committee are diverse and span the entirety of the project lifecycle and also include activities outside of the project environment. The Steering Committee will be involved in strategic planning and setting priorities for the organisation as a whole, as well as the selection and prioritisation of projects. They will be involved in resource allocation, similarly determining prioritisation where resources are constrained and/ or highly in demand (Kloppenborg, 2009). The guidance and assistance role of the sponsor also extends to the committee, who will provide feedback during project reviews and will otherwise offer support and encouragement as needed.

Monitoring and measuring progress through metrics and reports issued by the project leadership also forms a significant part of the committee's responsibilities. As with the sponsor, each member must have a suitable level of experience and authority to aid decision-making, including approval of change requests/ deviations and go/no go decisions at defined decision points (APM, 2019).

Project Management Office (PMO)

If an organisation is delivering many projects, there may be common governance and project management activities and reporting across its projects. A Project Management Office (PMO) is a centralised organisational function that provides support to projects, programmes, and portfolios. The PMO can act as a central repository for project management best practice (i.e. methodologies, tools, and techniques) and lessons learned for the organisation, which project managers can draw on to ensure the project has the best chance of success and to avoid each new project having to 'reinvent the wheel'. Further, a PMO allows the common work activities to be shared across projects, programmes, and portfolios, rather than resourcing for each individual endeavour. This may include (APM, 2019):

- Controls and reporting: collecting, analysing, and presenting progress information and managing interdependencies across projects.
- Assurance: conducting audits and reviews to support decision points and change control.
- Centre of excellence: improving project management processes, tools and techniques, embedding these through training and support, and measuring capabilities to review progress and target higher levels of competence and proficiency.
- Specialist support: providing specialist skills and expertise, such as risk, quality, planning, or finance, to both serve the project and benefit other project professionals.

- Information management: document management and access to information, tools, and services.

The role of the PMO varies considerably across organisations with regards to its degree of control and influence on projects, ranging from: (i) a supportive role, providing best practice and training; to (ii) a controlling role, checking compliance to project management frameworks and methodologies; to (iii) a directive role, whereby project managers are assigned by and report to the PMO (PMI, 2023).

Regardless of the nature of control from the PMO, one consistent factor for success is effective communication between the PMO and the projects' stakeholders (particularly the project sponsors and project managers). This principle applies equally to the Steering Committee and Project Sponsor.

Summary

This chapter has addressed how organisations select the right projects and ensure they are carried out in the right way. Selecting the right projects starts with the organisation's strategic planning, and the importance of aligning projects with the organisation's strategy cannot be overstated. Most organisations choose to structure their projects into programmes and portfolios—each of which satisfy a different strategic purpose—so as to maximise the benefit to the organisation.

Resources are often scarce, and not all projects can be funded. Project selection (and prioritisation) is essential, involving choosing those projects that are most closely aligned to the organisation's strategic aims and applying portfolio management in ensuring a balance of projects in the portfolio. This is an ongoing process beyond project selection, so as to ensure this alignment endures and that a project's priority within the portfolio remains appropriate in response to changing conditions. Away from strategic fit and portfolio balance, projects must also be scrutinised through effective governance to control the progress of projects through the stage gate process (most notably, at decision points). Governance also extends to support and oversight of activities, and the involvement of the Project Sponsor, Steering Committee, and PMO in which is particularly notable.

In the next chapter, we turn our attention to the first stage of the project lifecycle: Project Initiation.

References

APM (2011). *Directing Change: A Guide to Governance of Project Management* (3rd ed.), Princes Risborough: Association for Project Management.

APM (2019). *APM Body of Knowledge* (7th ed.), Princes Risborough: Association for Project Management.

Archer, N. and Ghasemzadeh, F. (2004). Project Portfolio Selection and Management. In: Morris, P.W.G. and Pinto, J. (eds.), *The Wiley Guide to Managing Projects*, Hoboken, NJ: Wiley. pp. 237–255.

Gavin, C.J. and Forsyth, S. (2021). *How to Be a Highly Effective Sponsor, Project*, Issue 307, Summer 2021. pp. 47–49.

Jamieson, A. and Morris, P.W.G. (2004). Moving from Corporate Strategy to Project Strategy. In: Morris, P.W.G. and Pinto, J. (eds.), *The Wiley Guide to Managing Projects*, Hoboken, NJ: Wiley. pp. 177–205.

Kloppenborg, T. (2009). *Project Management: A Contemporary Approach*, Mason, OH: South-Western Cengage Learning.

Kloppenborg, T., Anantatmula, V. and Wells, K.N. (2019). *Contemporary Project Management* (4th ed.), Boston, MA: Cengage Learning.

Larson, E.W. and Gray, C.F. (2018). *Project Management: The Managerial Process* (7th ed.), New York: McGraw-Hill Education.

Maylor, H. and Turner, N. (2022). *Project Management* (5th ed.), Harlow: Pearson.

Morris, P.W.G. (2013). *Reconstructing Project Management*, Chichester, UK: Wiley.

Nicholas, J.M. and Steyn, H. (2008). *Project Management for Business, Engineering and Technology: Principles and Practice* (3rd ed.), Oxford: Butterworth-Heinemann.

OECD (2004). *OECD Principles of Corporate Governance*, France: OECD Publications, www.oecd.org.

PMI (2021). *A Guide to the Project Management Body of Knowledge (PMBOK Guide)* (7th ed.), Newtown Square, PA: Project Management Institute.

PMI (2023). *Process Groups: A Practice Guide*, Newtown Square, PA: Project Management Institute.

Powell, M. and Young, J. (2004). The Project Management Support Office. In: Morris, P.W.G. and Pinto, J. (eds.), *The Wiley Guide to Managing Projects*, Hoboken, NJ: Wiley. pp. 937–982.

Thiry, M. (2004). Program Management: A Strategic Decision Management Process. In: Morris, P.W.G. and Pinto, J. (eds.), *The Wiley Guide to Managing Projects*, Hoboken, NJ: Wiley. pp. 257–287.

Wells, K. and Kloppenborg, T. (2015). *Project Management Essentials*, New York: Business Expert Press.

Wysocki, R.K. (2019). *Effective Project Management: Traditional, Agile, Extreme, Hybrid* (8th ed.), Indianapolis, IN: Wiley.

3   Project Initiating

Introduction

Within the project lifecycle, the first stage of any project is *Initiation.* It is here that the identified problem or opportunity is developed into a *business case,* which thereafter is scrutinised by the organisation's decision-makers with regards to the project's value and feasibility. If selected, the business case will then be developed further into a *project charter.* We will address each of these activities in turn.

Project Identification

Projects are created for a reason—a need that can be satisfied, a problem that can be solved, an opportunity that can be explored. The first challenge for an organisation is identifying this stimulus for a new project. Ideally, this is not something that happens purely by chance but rather is a result of strategic intent on the behalf of the organisation. Whilst some opportunities will present themselves, others will need to be searched for, and thus there should be a clear organisational process around the identification of potential projects. Given that projects are an excellent source of organisational transformation, new projects should be considered as part of the setting of the organisation's strategic objectives. It may also be desirable to form a group of employees to discuss market trends and potential projects, although better still is to involve everyone in

DOI: 10.4324/9781003057246-3

the organisation in this process: empowering all employees to propose new projects (particularly those whose roles involve contact with would-be stakeholders).

Beyond identification of the opportunity, the value of the potential project must also be examined at this early stage. This is to ensure that the organisation's resources are not expended on developing an idea into a business case (discussed subsequently) when it is simply not viable. As such, this step should also consider possible solutions to the problem/opportunity, the scale of the project (in terms of people, time, cost, etc.), the risks that would be entailed, and the extent to which this project would be complementary to the organisation's strategic objectives and the other projects and programmes in the organisation's portfolio. If given the green light, these considerations can be further expanded into a business case.

The Business Case

The business case is defined by APM (2019) as the "justification for undertaking a project, in terms of evaluating the benefits, costs and risks of alternative options and rationale for the preferred solution. […] It is owned by the sponsor." This definition, whilst useful, is, however, grounded in the assumption that benefits and costs can be estimated, risks can be assessed, the problem or opportunity is clearly understood, and a sponsor is assigned, which may not be the case (Maylor and Turner, 2022).

In addition to the desirability of the project (i.e. the combination of benefits, costs, and risks), the business case also attests to whether the project is (Murray, 2017):

- Viable: able to deliver the desired output(s).
- Achievable: use of the output(s) is likely to result in the envisaged outcomes and resulting benefits.

Given that we ultimately measure a project's success or failure by how well it addresses the identified problem or opportunity, it is vital that any project starts here. The temptation of many is to jump to immediately contemplating the solution before having fully understood the need for the project or what it is aiming to achieve. This can create a 'quality gap' between the requirements for the project and the proposed solution, which can be very difficult to rectify once the project is fully in motion, and can endure right through to the project close. As such, the first step in developing a business case is to develop a complete and accurate understanding of the problem or opportunity. Regardless of whether the customer of the project is internal or external to the organisation, it is vital that they are engaged with at this stage to develop a robust set of requirements that minimises the scope for misunderstanding and misinterpretation.

The requirements at this stage should be focused on the objectives of the organisation that the project will address and the metrics by which success can be measured (Maritato, 2013). These are our *business requirements* and should outline the needs of the whole organisation (rather than individual groups of stakeholders therein) and the business value that the project should deliver.

In just the same regard, project managers must be clear on the resource and budget constraints that the project will be subject to. Utilising experience is very important at this stage. Experience from past projects, both within and outside the organisation, will ultimately lead to estimates and considerations such as risks and constraints being reflected more realistically in the business case. Similarly, involving people other than the Project Manager in the formulation of the business case will mean it benefits from their past experience and encourages their commitment to the project at this early stage.

Hereafter, the solution, or solution options, are outlined, based on the identified requirements and constraints. This should include:

- *Costs:* consider both variable (dependent on the quantity of output generated, such as materials, supplies, fuel, and wages) and fixed costs (which remain the same regardless of the output generated, such as rent); and both direct (those directly associated with the project, such as materials and outsourcing) and indirect costs (which are incurred by multiple projects, such as the organisation's taxes, administration expenses, etc.). Sunk costs (i.e. those already incurred) should be ignored.

- *Benefits:* similarly, this should consider both direct reduced costs/savings (e.g. costs of human resources, IT, etc.) and benefits (e.g. increased sales) resulting from the project and indirect benefits (which cannot be directly observed, such as increased productivity, greater efficiency, etc.). Intangible benefits, which, whilst they cannot be quantified and thus will not form part of any cost-benefit calculation, should also be included here so as to provide further justification for the project (e.g. reduced reputational risk, increased staff morale, improved customer experience).
- *Assumptions*: it is important to also document the assumptions made around these costs and benefits. This will give an indication of the extent to which this assessment is reality, so as to provide a level of confidence in the details provided, and will also signal whether the assumption can be verified.
- *Risks:* an account of the risks associated with each option (refer to Chapter 4).
- *Constraints:* further to the resource and budget constraints identified earlier in the business case, there may also be constraints specific to each solution option. Also, the business case may need to consider the way in which existing projects in the organisation's portfolio might lead to limitations with regards to resources or affect the timing of the proposed project.

Financial Appraisal

A financial appraisal of the costs and benefits of each option should also be conducted (including the option to do nothing), so as to provide a basis for comparison across the options. There are several modes that this can take, using different indicators to measure the impact on the organisation's profitability and liquidity over time (and can also include non-financial and qualitative aspects). Along with providing a basis for comparison, it can also serve as a baseline for measuring success as the project advances. We will address three options for financial appraisal here, and whilst this set of approaches is certainly not exhaustive, these are among the most common:

• Payback period (PBP)
• Net present value (NPV)
• Internal rate of return (IRR)

As will be seen, each addresses different aspects of profitability, liquidity, and risk in assessing and comparing solution options. The decision of which of these methods to use in providing a basis for evaluation and analysis will ultimately depend on the size of the project and the timespan over which the benefits and costs will be spread.

Payback Period (PBP)

PBP is the most basic mode of financial appraisal, calculating the period of time (typically months and years) that the project will take to repay its initial investment. As such, it focuses on cash flows (i.e. revenue and costs) across a time period until the project's initial investment has been recouped. An example is shown in Example 3.1.

Whilst simple to calculate, payback period does not address the time value of money (described subsequently). It also only considers costs within the payback period and therefore does not represent reality for projects with high costs at the end of the lifecycle (e.g. decommissioning costs for engineering projects) and otherwise encourages short-term thinking. These shortcomings are addressed to varying degrees by the alternative approaches described hereafter.

Example 3.1 Payback Period

The project requires an initial investment of £50,000 and is expected to generate the following cash flows over the next five years.

Year	Initial Investment	Revenue	Costs	Cash Flow	Cumulative Cash Flow (CCF)
0	50,000	—	—	−50,000	−50,000
1		20,000	25,000	−5,000	−55,000
2		30,000	25,000	5,000	−50,000
3		35,000	25,000	10,000	−40,000
4		45,000	30,000	15,000	−25,000
5		60,000	30,000	30,000	5,000
Total	**50,000**	**185,000**	**135,000**		

We can see from this that the project will breakeven sometime in Year 5. To calculate this more precisely, we can use a simple calculation:

$PBP = A + (B/C)$, where A is the year of the first positive cumulative cash flow, B is the absolute value (i.e. without a negative sign) of the CCF for the year preceding Year A (i.e. the last year with a negative cumulative cash flow), and C is the cash flow for Year A.

$$PBP = 5 + (25,000/30,000) = 5.83 \text{ Years}$$

Net Present Value (NPV)

NPV represents the value today of the project's future cash flows. This involves discounting all future net cash flows with a discount rate, resulting in a discounted cash flow. The sum of these discounted cash flows is the NPV for the project.

Example 3.2 Net Present Value

NPV = PV of benefits − PV of costs,
        where PV = $C_n/(1 + i)^n$
        C_n = future of investment, *n* years hence
        i = discount rate

Therefore, if a project requires a £50,000 investment now and will yield £85,000 over the next five years, the NPV against a discount rate of 5% will be:

PV of benefits	= $85,000/(1 + 0.05)^5$
	= 85,000/1.34
	= 63,432.84
PV of costs	= 50,000
NPV	= 63,432.84 − 50,000
	= 13,432.84

If given the choice between receiving £1,000 now, or £1,000 a year from now, most people would choose to receive the money now so that it could be invested and benefit from interest rates. If invested over several years, interest would be paid on the original £1,000 plus interest accrued in subsequent years: a phenomenon known as compound interest.

Conversely, when borrowing money, interest is accrued not only on the capital amount but also on any unpaid interest.

Discounting avoids this compounding effect by assessing the project's value in today's terms: the present value (PV). As such, it considers the opportunity cost in making an investment— sometimes termed the 'time value of money'—that comes from not doing something else with the resources. The minimum to be expected from a project is that the NPV be greater than zero against the given discount rate (anything greater than zero will be profit).

Example 3.3 Net Present Value with Discount Rate

The costs and revenues associated with the project are shown below. It is to be assessed against a discount rate of 10% over a period of three years.

	Now	Year 1	Year 2	Year 3
Start-up costs	50,000			
Running costs				
(rent, rates, wages)		25,000	45,000	50,000
Revenues		30,000	60,000	110,000

$$\begin{aligned} NPV &= NPV \text{ (Year 1)} + NPV \text{ (Year 2)} + NPV \text{ (Year 3)} \\ &= (-50,000) + (-25,000 + 30,000)/(1 + 0.10)^1 + \\ &\quad (-45,000 + 60,000)/(1 + 0.10)^2 + (-50,000 + \\ &\quad 110,000)/(1 + 0.10)^3 \\ &= -50,000 + 4,545.45 + 12,396.69 + 45,079.89 \\ &= 12,021.04 \end{aligned}$$

Example 3.2 shows the effect of time on benefits, but this can also be applied to the effect on costs over time (where a project requires not only an initial investment but also ongoing expenditure over time).

A discount rate, for either costs or benefits, could be the interest rate that would be accrued from the bank, although more commonly a higher rate is applied so that it is harder for projects to meet the minimum criterion of an NPV of zero. Maylor and Turner (2022) suggest that the discount rate should consider:

(a) The interest rate charged for the use of the capital.
(b) The inflation rate (so as to account for the change in purchasing power).
(c) A premium factor to account for the return expected by the investor on the project, or the risk for the investor that the capital may never be repaid.

Thus, the discount rate $= (1 + a) \times (1 + b) \times (1 + c)$

Projects will typically involve varying revenues and costs over a period of several years, as shown in the more complex example (Example 3.3).

Although NPV examines the cash flows throughout the life of the project, the discounting effect reduces the impact of long-term (and thus *less certain*) revenues and costs. In the same regard, it is also very sensitive to the initial investment cost. A key challenge comes in determining the discount rate against which the NPV be assessed. If a rate of 15% was applied to the example above, the NPV would more than half. A rate of 20% would see it fall to less than zero (and would thus be rejected).

Internal Rate of Return (IRR)

Related to NPV is the calculation of the IRR of a project: the discount rate at which NPV is zero. This can be achieved by experimenting with different discount rates in a manner that gradually arrives at a result of NPV = 0. For the example above, we know that the IRR lies somewhere between 15% and 20%, and through a process of trial-and-error, we could arrive at a more accurate indication of the IRR of the project. This process of trial-and-error, with NPVs for various discount rates, can also be used to plot a curve on a graph to aid in identifying exactly at which rate NPV = 0.

Like NPV, it can be a useful basis for comparing various project options, with the highest IRR indicating the most favourable (and a strong candidate for investment, if that IRR is higher than current and forecasted interest rates). The process also benefits from removing the need to decide on a discount rate. It nevertheless has some drawbacks. Most notably, it cannot account for changes in the discount rate over time. Further, organisations must be wary of using IRR in isolation, as two options with the same IRR can have very different NPVs. Whilst an appraisal of a project using both NPV and IRR will typically result in the same accept or reject decision, when comparing several options, it can lead to options being ranked quite differently. As such, it is suggested that, for most projects, a combination of these modes of financial appraisal are used in support of the decision-making process.

Cost-Benefit Analysis

The financial appraisal is one crucial part of a broader assessment of the costs and benefits of the project solution options (i.e. a cost-benefit analysis). Whereas the financial appraisal examines quantitative strengths and weaknesses of each option, there will be further qualitative considerations. These may include benefits such as increased process efficiency, customer satisfaction, and quality of products and services. There will be qualitative disadvantages in just the same regard, in terms of level of risk and non-economic factors (e.g. social or ecological impact, or brand image). It may be possible to quantify some of these qualitative considerations into financial benefits or cash flow equivalents; with others, it will not. Regardless, it is important that all quantitative and qualitative factors are communicated as part of the cost-benefit analysis. These can then be consolidated and compared across each of the project options.

Ultimately, the completion of the cost-benefit analysis should lead to a recommendation (and potentially discarding some options), based on and justified by the evaluation of the financial and qualitative factors. This should include details of how the chosen option should be undertaken, and the key individuals, resources, and actions required to do so.

With the business case finalised, two important questions should have clear and evidenced answers:

- Can we do it?—can the project be carried out with the available resources, alongside the projects already in the portfolio?
- Should we do it?—having assessed the costs and risks of the project, and its anticipated benefits, should the project be carried out?

Hereafter, the business case must be treated as a living document that is maintained throughout the project's life. It should be reviewed regularly, one reason for which is to ensure the justification for the project remains as robust as at the point of sign-off. If the justification for the project has fallen away—perhaps due to more attractive propositions becoming available—then it should be halted, where possible. Many of the details within will also be valuable in appraising the project's progress beyond the Initiation stage.

Strategic Misrepresentation and Optimism Bias

When assessing a business case's merits, we must be mindful of the ways in which strategic misrepresentation and optimism bias can challenge the validity and reliability of its estimates. Professor Bent Flyvbjerg—an economic geographer—has conducted considerable research into this area, finding extensive evidence of both across several key economic sectors. In one study spanning several hundred projects in more than 20 countries, Flyvbjerg found that it is not necessarily the best projects that get chosen but rather those where their proponents are most successful in "conjuring a fantasy world of underestimated costs, overestimated revenues, undervalued environmental impacts and overvalued regional development effects" (Flyvbjerg, 2005). This effect can be the result of either conscious (as with strategic misrepresentation) or unconscious acts (as with optimism bias) on the behalf of the project's proponents.

Cost overruns and benefit shortfalls ultimately lead to inefficient allocation of resources (i.e. waste), delays, and further cost overruns and benefit shortfalls, which can destabilise planning, implementation, and operations of projects. This has become a bigger problem in the wider project community as projects have increased in scale and scope (Flyvbjerg, 2007a). In some cases, the exaggeration of benefits and underestimation of costs can not only lead to financial difficulties but can also extend to influencing the safety of the project output.

Three types of explanations have been offered by researchers (summarised in Flyvbjerg, 2007a):

- Technical explanations, stemming from imperfect forecasting methods, honest mistakes, inadequate data, lack of experience in forecasting, etc.
- Psychological explanations, such as optimism bias or the planning fallacy (where project personnel make decisions based on delusional optimism rather than rational consideration).
- Political-economic explanations, whereby project leaders intentionally "spin scenarios of success and gloss over the potential for failure." This is a deliberate act, whereas optimism bias is not. Strategic misrepresentation is one example and is somewhat commonplace in organisations where there is competition for resources and deceiving decision-makers about a project's prospects may carry political and/or economic benefits for individuals.

It should be noted that whilst technical explanations gained widespread credence some time ago, they have largely been disproven through further research (Flyvbjerg, 2007a). Psychological and political-economic explanations have been found to be much better explanations for the phenomenon of cost overruns and benefit shortfalls.

Clearly this calls for greater scrutiny to be placed on the forecasts established at this stage of a project's life. One solution is to utilise independent specialists to appraise the costs, benefits, and risks detailed in the business case. Another lies in utilising the experience of similar, past projects, and one approach—'reference case forecasting' (refer to Lovallo and Kahneman, 2003)—is particularly effective in improving accuracy of forecasts. The approach utilises data from comparable projects to establish a probability distribution for project outcomes, siting the project within that distribution. The existing forecasts can then be assessed for reliability and corrected accordingly (termed 'optimism uplift'). Adopting this 'outside view' in forecasting has been shown to be much more accurate than the consistently optimistic 'inside view' (APM, 2018).

The dark arts of strategic misrepresentation are somewhat harder to address and call for an organisation, and moreover governments where taxpayer money is at stake, to establish strong governance, assurance, and accountability over the actions of project personnel. This can take the form of auditing, reviewing, benchmarking, and critically questioning the forecasts put forward, with penalties in place to enforce deception and, conversely, incentives to reward valid forecasts (detailed further in Flyvbjerg, 2007b).

All this is not to suggest that optimism on a project is a bad thing. Optimism is a vital part of driving a project forward with enthusiasm, instilling project personnel with a sense of meaning and purpose over their work. In this regard, it should be encouraged. However, in determining forecasts of costs, benefits, and risks of a project, this must make way for objectivity and realism.

Project Evaluation and Selection

As described in Chapter 2, this is the process of evaluating individual projects, or comparing projects, and then deciding whether a project will proceed to the Planning stage on the basis that it will support the organisation in achieving its objectives. These objectives might be purely financial, some of the measures of which are described above, but many organisations consider the wider issue of organisational value, whereby measures such as customer satisfaction, brand awareness, and process efficiency also form part of this evaluation process. Equally, there may be a need to assess not only the costs and benefits of the project but also the opportunity cost of not doing the project.

Rather than being a single event, organisations should continuously evaluate and select projects in recognition that new projects are proposed, older projects reach the end of their lifecycle (or are cancelled), new market opportunities arise, and internal resources increase or decrease in capacity.

The role of the PMO (for those organisations with a PMO; discussed in Chapter 2) is crucial here as the centralised decision-making body for the organisation. It is the PMO, with its top-down perspective over the organisation's entire project portfolio, that is best placed to understand how the project being proposed aligns with the objectives of the wider organisation and might impact or complement the projects already in motion. In smaller organisations, this role can be performed by an individual Portfolio Manager.

Project Charter

Once a project has been selected, a *project charter* must be drawn up. The charter has several important purposes. The first is to establish a common understanding of what the project entails and the rationale or justification for it (including how this aligns with the ongoing work of the organisation). Secondly, it outlines the project scope, objectives, and anticipated benefits; the estimates of its costs and risks; and any key milestones and approval requirements. Finally, the signing of the project charter provides written authorisation to the Project Manager to proceed with the project.

The charter can serve as a final sense check. The Project Manager should now be in a strong position to clearly outline what the project is and why it matters, but if that is not the case, the charter will highlight this. Similarly with questions like "what does success look like?", "who is responsible for X and Y?", or "who are the key stakeholders?". This final process and the act of signing off can highlight persistent problems and ensure things proceed with a clear focus and vision. If agreement cannot be reached, the project may need to be amended or even aborted. Better to do so now than proceed when such issues persist.

3 Ws	**What** (scope)	**Why** (business case)	**When** (milestones, schedule, & acceptance criteria)
3 Rs	**Risks**	**Resources**	**Routines**
3 Cs	**Communication needs** (stakeholders)	**Collection of knowledge** (lessons learned)	**Commitment** (sign-off)

Figure 3.1 The Three Ws, Rs, and Cs of Project Charters.

Source: Wells and Kloppenborg, 2015.

Wells and Kloppenborg (2015) provide a useful framework for the components of a typical project charter (Figure 3.1).

The *What* section addresses the scope—as in both what the project does and does not include. The *Why* section addresses the justification for the project—a short summary of the business case (i.e. what are the objectives of the project, and why does it matter). The *When* addresses milestones and acceptance criteria, and these two are distinct. Milestones are achievements along the project lifecycle, used to acknowledge progress against the ultimate goal (e.g. completion of a deliverable, drafting of a plan, etc.). These are accompanied by acceptance criteria against which progress will be measured, so that we can highlight shortfalls but also celebrate successes. For example, for the milestone of "Quality Assurance Schedule drafted," the acceptance criteria might be: (i) key roles and responsibilities assigned; (ii) shared and agreed with key stakeholders; (iii) signed-off by project management.

Risks will be addressed much further in Chapter 4. On the charter specifically, risks includes both threats and opportunities (e.g. any event that may happen, how likely it is to happen, and what its impact might be). Constraints and assumptions also often fall into this category, as per the PMI's guidance (2021, 2023). *Resources,* discussed much further in Chapter 5, encapsulates all the human, financial, and other resources that will be required by the project. *Routines* describes how the team will work effectively together (e.g. decision-making, minimising conflict, building trust, etc.).

Communication needs will firstly identify the project's key stakeholders and thereafter address their expectations with regards to communication (addressed further in Chapter 6). *Collection of knowledge* outlines how the project plans to learn from the past experiences of other projects and translate these into actions, and, conversely, how lessons learned will be captured as the project proceeds. Whilst consolidating lessons learned is a crucial part of closing a project (refer to Chapter 8), it should not be left until the last minute, and thus the charter should establish prior to the Planning stage how it will be managed. Finally, *Commitment* is where the Project Sponsor, Project Manager, and other key project team personnel sign off their commitment to the project.

The level of detail required in each of these categories to assure the project's authorities that the project is ready to proceed to the Planning stage will vary depending on the size of the project. And of course, more detail around each of these areas will be planned for and documented in the subsequent stage. On some larger projects, and something particularly common with major engineering projects, clear plans are required to be in place before sign-off, and thus a project initiation document (PID) is used.

Project Initiation Document (PID)

The PID serves a similar purpose to the project charter—its core function is to attain and record written commitment for the project to proceed to the Planning stage—but typically has more detail. This may include:

- *Project Background:* a description of why and how the project was created.
- *Initial Project Plan:* including key phases, milestones, deadlines, etc.

- *Communication Plan:* modes of communication and the accountable personnel, along with stakeholder expectations (and how these will be met and by whom).
- *Quality Plan:* details of the quality targets for the project, and the assurance and control measures that will be in place in pursuit of these.
- *Project Controls:* an account of how (e.g. key performance indicators) and when (i.e. a schedule) project progress will be measured, monitored, and reported.
- *Risk Register and Management Plan:* key risks are identified, and a plan formulated for their mitigation.

Ultimately, whichever of these is used—the project charter or the PID—is a decision made by the organisation. For some smaller projects, the Planning stage is not so costly that planning for considerations such as communication, quality, risk, etc. cannot be left until this subsequent stage; for others, requiring multi-billion US$ investment, early plans need to be in place to provide assurance that the project will efficiently utilise resources in the Planning stage (where these plans will be further honed and will continue to evolve as the project proceeds).

Summary

Projects are highly valuable to organisations, not only as a source of revenue but also as a source for change. Operating under finite resources, few organisations can afford to choose the wrong project (nor reject the right one), and this is why the Project Initiating stage is of such importance. Merrow (2011) describes it as the weakest stage for most project organisations: some bad ideas enter the Planning stage, and some of those bad ideas become real projects.

We have discussed the ways in which potential projects are first identified and then how the requirements of that project can be effectively collected and communicated. Hereafter, a business case is built around these requirements, at which point the constraints, risks, and benefits are outlined, and a robust statement of the project's value is recorded. A cost-benefit analysis (including a financial appraisal) provides further evidence of the feasibility and value of the project. We further discussed the process of evaluation and selection, and, if selected, how the commitment to the project is attained and recorded with a project charter (or project initiation document).

We now turn our attention to the Planning stage. We first examine the process of scoping a project in Chapter 4, before the two subsequent chapters address resource planning and stakeholder and communication management, respectively.

References

APM (2018). *De-risking the Programme Portfolio with Reference Class Forecasting* [Online]. Available: www.apm.org.uk/news/de-risking-the-programme-portfolio-with-reference-class-forecasting/ [Accessed 3 February 2024].

APM (2019). *APM Body of Knowledge* (7th ed.), Princes Risborough: Association for Project Management.

Flyvbjerg, B. (2005). Machiavellian Megaprojects, *Antipode*, 31(1), pp. 1822.

Flyvbjerg, B. (2007a). How Optimism Bias and Strategic Misrepresentation in Early Project Development Undermine Implementation, *Concept Report no. 17*, pp. 41–55.

Flyvbjerg, B. (2007b). Eliminating Bias in Early Project Development through Reference Class Forecasting and Good Governance, *Concept Report no. 17*, pp. 90–110.

Lovallo, D. and Kahneman, D. (2003). Delusions of Success: How Optimism Undermines Executives' Decisions, *Harvard Business Review*, July, pp. 56–63.

Maritato, M. (2013). Mastering the Project Requirements. Paper presented at *PMI Global Congress 2013-EMEA*, Istanbul, Turkey. Newtown Square, PA: Project Management Institute.

Maylor, H. and Turner, N. (2022). *Project Management* (5th ed.), Harlow: Pearson.

Merrow, E.W. (2011). *Industrial Megaprojects: Concepts, Strategies, and Practices for Success*, Hoboken, NJ: Wiley.

Murray, A. (2017). *Managing Successful Projects with PRINCE2* (6th ed.), London: The Stationary Office.

PMI (2021). *A Guide to the Project Management Body of Knowledge (PMBOK Guide)* (7th ed.), Newtown Square, PA: Project Management Institute.

PMI (2023). *Process Groups: A Practice Guide*, Newtown Square, PA: Project Management Institute.

Wells, K. and Kloppenborg, T. (2015). *Project Management Essentials*, New York: Business Expert Press.

4 Project Planning

Scope of Work

Introduction

Planning is key to project success. One quote we are particularly fond of—not from an academic but from a former student—is that *projects don't go wrong, they start wrong*. As such, we will dedicate the next three chapters to project planning, the first of which here will focus on how to develop a scope of work and how to plan for issues around complexity, risk, and uncertainty thereafter.

There are several important reasons why we project plan, as outlined by Kuster et al. (2015). Whilst we should already have a robust set of requirements if we have approached Project Initiation in the manner described in the preceding chapter, the project plan is a further opportunity to ensure these requirements are complete, clear, and realistic. This is the scope of work—what is included and what is not included in the project. From here, we can build a structure around individual deliverables and 'work packages' that comprise the project, placing clear boundaries between them so that responsibilities can be assigned. We can also consider bottlenecks and conflicts with regards to resources at this early stage (resources such as people, money, machinery, etc.), so that any corrective action can be taken now so as to minimise disruption in project execution (addressed in Chapter 5). It also clearly communicates to everyone involved what will be delivered, by whom, and when.

DOI: 10.4324/9781003057246-4

Finally, it creates a baseline against which the project's actual status can be measured as it moves through the lifecycle.

Building a Scope of Work

The process of project planning must start with the requirements. The importance of having a complete and clear set of *business requirements* was discussed in the context of the business case in Chapter 3. Having recognised the value to the business that the project promises, we must now continue to gather requirements from stakeholders, as well as the requirements for the chosen solution and how it will be implemented. As with the Initiating stage, this is a pivotal first step from which all further activities are built. For instance, the Standish Group's (2004) CHAOS Report found that three of the top five reasons that projects fail involve requirements (cited in Coventry, 2015):

• Users are not sufficiently involved in requirements definition.
• Requirements are incomplete or do not meet acceptance criteria.
• Requirements are constantly changing, and these changes are not managed effectively.

Requirements should be gathered and managed in the Planning stage at three different levels (Maritato, 2013):

• *Stakeholder Requirements:* the needs of a stakeholder or class of stakeholders, including how they will interact with the solution. It is for the Project Manager to understand these and select the ones that will be implemented in the project. If a stakeholder requirement cannot be traced back to a business requirement, it is a good candidate for exclusion from the project;
• *Solution Requirements:* the characteristics of the solution (both functional and non-functional) that meet both the stakeholder requirements and business requirements. These

must be identified before the technical solution is selected as they will ultimately support the selection or the design of the technical solution and how it will be implemented;

- *Transition Requirements:* the capabilities that the solution must provide in order to transition the organisation from the current state to a desired future state. Can only be described once the new solution has been designed and will be determined by the 'readiness' of the organisation to implement the new solution: the more 'ready' the organisation is, the fewer transition requirements will be required.

With regards to stakeholder requirements, there is an opportunity here to introduce new methods of gathering requirements, which can be valuable in both addressing any remaining uncertainty around what exactly the customer wants and engaging stakeholders in discussions around the feasibility and impact of certain requirements (i.e. in terms of cost, schedule, quality, etc.). This could include, for example, questionnaires, mind mapping sessions, interviews with stakeholders, observation, focus groups, and prototyping (Wells and Kloppenborg, 2015). This process can also establish in new project members (and reinforce in existing members) a clear picture of what the project is, why it is being undertaken, and who the key stakeholders are.

The Project Manager must ensure that any new or revised requirements are clear, specific, measurable, and verifiable. They should also be realistic. Whilst a project should aim to meet or exceed a customer's (and other stakeholder's) expectations, these expectations must be realistic. Where this is not the case, it is best to address these now with the stakeholder(s) rather than setting the project up to disappoint. Now would also be a good time to revisit the assumptions and constraints previously outlined in the business case to ensure these do not require updating.

The solution and transition requirements describe the solution and how it will implemented, whereas the stakeholder and

Business/ Stakeholder Requirement	Solution/ Transition Requirement	Stakeholder(s)	Priority

Figure 4.1 Requirements Traceability Matrix (Adapted from Wells and Kloppenborg, 2015).

business requirements describe the value of the project to its stakeholders and the organisation. It is important that the former are traced back to the latter and that this is documented. For larger, more complex projects, a *Requirements Management Plan* and *Requirements Traceability Matrix* can be developed in support of this. The former describes how requirements will be gathered, analysed, categorised and prioritised, and shared amongst the project's stakeholders. The latter simply maps the business/stakeholder requirements to individual solution/transition requirements in a matrix and can include details of the stakeholder from whom the requirement came and a priority level. Prioritisation can be based upon multiple dimensions, such as business value, business/technical risk, difficulty of implementation, likelihood of success, regulatory/policy compliance, stakeholder agreement, and urgency (IIBA, 2009). An example template is shown in Figure 4.1.

Once satisfied that the requirements are complete, these must be developed into a set of deliverables that the project team will produce over the lifecycle of the project in order to meet these requirements. This is the first step of the planning stage, with all further activities—such as assigning resources, building a schedule, identifying risks, and stakeholder planning—developed from this set of deliverables. The scope of work must comprise: the deliverables that will be handed over to the customer and the work activities required to produce these deliverables. As with the requirements, every deliverable should be clear, specific, measurable, and verifiable. These are often represented graphically in a set of breakdown structures: the deliverables in a *product breakdown structure (PBS)* and the work activities in a *work breakdown structure (WBS). The organisational breakdown structure (OBS)*—which represents the structure of project organisation with its various departments and organisational functions—is discussed in Chapter 5.

Product Breakdown Structure (PBS)

A PBS is a hierarchical structure of the deliverables that the project will produce and deliver within the project's lifecycle, broken down into its constituent parts. The PBS can often become confused with the WBS, but there is an important distinction between them. Every component of the PBS must be a deliverable, conveyed as either a noun or an outcome in the past tense (e.g. "Testing Plan" or "Training Delivered"). It should not reference 'work' (e.g. "Install Plumbing"): if it does, it should be converted to a product (APM, n.d.). An example PBS is shown in Figure 4.2, taken from a recent campervan conversion project of one of the authors.

Work Breakdown Structure (WBS)

Whilst they may look similar, the PBS and WBS serve different functions in the planning process. Whilst the PBS outlines everything that will be produced by a project, the WBS describes all the activities that will need to be performed to create those products. Put simply, the PBS shows where we are going, and the WBS tells us how to get there. As such, the PBS precedes (and feeds into the creation of) the WBS.

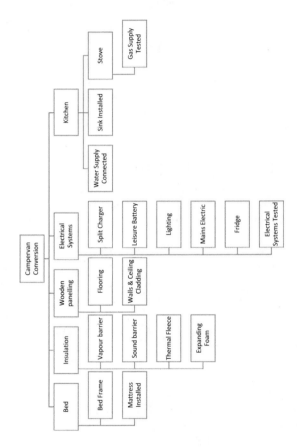

Figure 4.2 Product Breakdown Structure (Authors' Own).

Projects are divided and subdivided into manageable blocks, termed *work packages*, and subdivided further thereafter into sub-activities until you arrive at a level that is small enough to manage: a rule of thumb proposed by Wells and Kloppenborg (2015) is that the lowest-level activities should be able to be completed by one person in one day. Moreover, 'the 100% rule' (Haugan, 2002) is an important guiding principle in developing a WBS: first, the whole WBS should include 100% of the work to be delivered on the project; secondly, this rule applies at all levels of the hierarchy, with the sum of the work at the 'child' level accounting for 100% of the work at the 'parent' level; and, finally, the WBS should not include more than 100% of the work (i.e. any work that falls outside the scope of the project).

This process of subdivision will ultimately simplify the management of these activities later on when we come to build a schedule and plan the allocation of resources around these activities. Components here should be conveyed as a verb and a noun (e.g. "Develop Testing Plan" or "Deliver Training"). The structure is not representative of the order in which the activities will be performed: this will be determined later by the schedule.

An example WBS from the same campervan conversion project is shown in Figure 4.3.

Both the PBS and the WBS should be compiled in careful consideration of the project requirements. There should be traceability between the requirements and the PBS and WBS and between the PBS and WBS. For instance, if an activity on the WBS cannot be traced to a product on the PBS, this can indicate that either unnecessary work is being planned, or that something is missing from the PBS.

Formalising Project Scope and Managing Change

The scope will continue to develop and become further defined as the project moves ahead through the planning stage and more detail unfolds (which will in turn allow for the above break-down structures to be further subdivided). Morris (1994), for

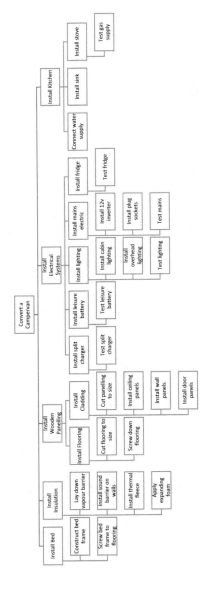

Figure 4.3 Work Breakdown Structure (Authors' Own).

instance, described the 'rolling wave' of knowledge in project planning, whereby the initial high-level assumptions and milestones give way to more accurate and detailed information over the course of the planning stage (termed the 'progressive elaboration of detail'). However, at some point, the scope will need to be baselined—the formal acceptance of the scope—so that we can start to schedule and allocate resources to the activities therein.

A *Project Scope Statement* is an effective way of formalising the project's scope and establishing a baseline at a given point in time. It will be published and shared amongst the project team, who will use it hereafter to plan and measure project success. The plan will typically include: the project's problem statement and key goals and objectives; a statement of requirements; the project deliverables (stemming from, and possibly including, the PBS and WBS); and the acceptance criteria against which we can measure that the requirements have been met and deliverables are correct.

Once the baseline has been established, the scope is frozen (at least in linear project management), and any changes to or deviations from this must be managed and documented. This is termed the *Change Control* process.

Change is an inevitable part of projects, as we have already discussed. What we are trying to avoid is unauthorised or uncontrolled change, often termed 'scope creep'. Scope creep describes the tendency for a project's scope to expand over time, with, for example, requirements and product features being added, or unauthorised work being carried out. It can often lead to inflation of costs, missed deadlines, or compromised quality of work (consider the discussion of the Project Management Triangle in Chapter 1). The process of baselining and formalising agreement to the scope is, in part, intended to prevent scope creep. A robust scope management process, encompassing change control, will equally be very important. Whilst change is a part of any project, the problems associated with scope creep in fact refer to unauthorised change, thus underlining the need for a formalised process with clear responsibilities.

The most important part of the *Change Control* process is the method of documenting changes. Changes are normally documented through a *Change Request,* described in the PMI guidance (PMI, 2021, 2023) as a written "request to expand or reduce the project scope, modify policies, processes, plans or procedures, modify costs or budgets, or revise schedules". Changes are formally proposed, and then a decision is made as to whether to approve the change. Only formally documented changes should be considered, and only approved changes should be implemented.

Projects sometimes fall down in only managing major changes or in only considering the primary (i.e. direct) impact of proposed changes. Collectively, minor changes can have a very significant impact over a project's chances of success, especially when we consider the secondary impacts.

Most organisations' approaches to change management address only the primary impact of a proposed change: i.e. the anticipated direct impact to budget or schedule in particular. However, there are secondary impacts that can have a very significant bearing on not only the project's success but also that of other projects within the organisation's portfolio. Cooper and Lee (2009) offer the example of a fairly simple change, such as adding a component to an engineering system, which comes with a modest impact to the budget in terms of the material cost of the component and some overtime to install it. However, if this is one of a hundred similar changes, all of which require overtime, what impact might this have on productivity, or the occurrence of errors due to fatigue? What might the knock-on effect to the schedule be (rather than just the direct impact) if this system is part of a delicately balanced sequence of work? If manpower is diverted to this project in order to meet this demand for rework, what impact might this have on the productivity of other projects in the portfolio? Secondary impacts occur far later in time and can be much harder to quantify than primary impacts, but they should nevertheless be built into the project's change control process given their potential significance to project success and organisational performance.

Complexity, Uncertainty, and Risk

Complexity, risk, and uncertainty are three very important terms for project management. As terms they are sometimes conflated, and within organisations, complexity, risks, and uncertainties can be mis-categorised as one another, leading to them being mismanaged. We focus now on clearly defining each term, drawing a distinction between them, so that we can also address approaches for their effective management.

Complexity

Complexity exists in every project to varying degrees. Merrow and Nandurdikar (2018) identify three sources of complexity on projects:

- *Scope Complexity*, which is derived from the number of elements within a project's scope. Large, complex projects may comprise a number of sub-projects, organised by distinctly different components of scope. For example, a new aircraft system will comprise the scope of work for the vehicle itself, alongside sub-projects for training, testing, procurement, maintenance, etc. The project operates as a system, with a set of components that must interact together in order for the system to function and create value.
- *Organisational Complexity,* which stems from scope complexity. Taking the aircraft system example, this would be best organised as a set of sub-teams, each developing and executing the necessary work to fulfil the scope of the respective sub-project. Each sub-team will have its own requirements with regards to expertise, its own leadership, and equally its own culture and working practices. For the complex project leader, line-of-sight management is not practicable (as it would otherwise be on a simple project) due to the number of individuals and organisations involved. Therefore, they must adopt the role of "leader of leaders": integrating the activities of the collective sub-projects to ensure the functioning of the system.

- *Shaping Complexity*, which derives from the involvement of stakeholders on a project. The involvement of stakeholders in the development of the project scope is commonplace on complex projects, and it is through this process that stakeholders are allocated value on a project and become aligned with its scope. This can include both internal stakeholders (e.g. company functions with a degree of control over the project) and external stakeholders (such as supply chain partners, contractors, government actors, etc.). Typically, the larger the project, the greater the number and diversity of stakeholders (and thus the greater the complexity and the greater the leadership challenge).

There are various organisational tools and actions that can be adopted by project teams in service of reducing and/or managing complexity of these three modes. These are summarised in Figure 4.4 and are detailed elsewhere in this book.

Scope Complexity	Organisational Complexity	Shaping Complexity
• Detailed planning (Chapter 4) • Product breakdown structure (Chapter 4) • Work breakdown structure (Chapter 4) • Change management (Chapter 4) • Risk Management (Chapter 4)	• Organisational breakdown structure (Chapter 5) • RACI (Chapter 5) • Cost breakdown structure and detailed Budgeting (Chapter 5) • Effective communication and strong interpersonal skills (Chapter 6)	• Stakeholder management (Chapter 6) • RACI (for internal stakeholders; Chapter 5) • Communication plan (Chapter 6) • Effective communication and strong interpersonal skills (Chapter 6)

Figure 4.4 Complexity Tools and Actions.

An extensive body of research over the last two decades has established the overwhelming conclusion that effective leadership is vital to project success (e.g. Turner and Muller, 2005; Yang et al., 2011; Nixon et al., 2012). With complex projects, the challenge for leaders is amplified, as is the importance of effective leadership to the success of such projects. Merrow and Nandurdikar (2018) argue that large, complex projects are in many regards fundamentally different to smaller, simpler projects, with leadership the defining factor in the success of the former:

> Our point is a simple one: the complex project leader's job is really quite difficult, and the skill set required to navigate this position well is quite remarkable. [...] As projects become more complex, the leadership role not only expands, it becomes progressively more important to project success. The complex project has many more paths to failure than a simple project. There are many more groups and individuals who can derail a complex project and it is less likely that all those groups and individuals are fully aligned around the definition of success of the project. [...] Complexity makes the project leader's job bigger, more varied, and more difficult.

Viewing projects as systems, complex projects are inherently more difficult to lead due to their large number of interacting elements. These systems are dynamic, with elements evolving from one another and with the environment, and minor changes can produce disproportionately major consequences (Snowden and Boone, 2007). It is therefore very difficult (or even impossible) to forecast or predict what will happen with any certainty on a complex project.

Given the unique challenge that complex projects pose, one crucial failure of project leadership is in relying on common leadership practices, treating complex projects as if they were simple. Whilst simple projects are characterised by predictability and order, complex projects are not and thus must be managed in different ways. Part of the leadership challenge lies in identifying the degree of complexity in a project, then adjusting behaviours and working practices accordingly.

In support of this, Snowden and Boone (2007) developed the Cynefin framework (pronounced *ku-nev-in*: a Welsh word meaning 'habitat' or 'environment') as a tool to help leaders determine the context they are operating in and to make appropriate choices based on that context. The authors outline five contexts, as defined by the nature of the relationship between cause and effect, with each requiring a different response from project leaders:

- *Simple Contexts—The Domain of Best Practice.* These contexts are characterised by stability and clear relationships between cause and effect that are easy to discern by all. The right answer is often self-evident and undisputed, and it requires straightforward management and monitoring. Leaders should sense (i.e. assess the facts around the situation), categorise them, and then respond as per best practice.
- *Complicated Contexts—The Domain of Experts.* These contexts may contain multiple right answers, and whilst there is a clear relationship between cause and effect, it will not be perceptible to all. Here, leaders should sense, *analyse*, and respond, and it is this process of analysis that calls for the involvement of experts in gaining a clearer, more accurate picture of the context so that the appropriate choices can be made. As this context calls for considering many options— several of which may be fit-for-purpose—it is defined by good practice, rather than best practice.
- *Complex Contexts—The Domain of Emergence.* These contexts are characterised by change, uncertainty, and unpredictability. There are no right answers available, and leaders must therefore probe (i.e. ask questions, stimulate discussion and interaction, experiment, etc.), sense (i.e. perceive patterns that emerge over time and determine which are desirable), and then respond by creating an environment

in which solutions can emerge. Leaders must be patient in allowing the path forward to reveal itself, rather than imposing a certain course of action.

- *Chaotic Contexts—The Domain of Rapid Response.* These contexts are characterised not only by change, uncertainty, and unpredictability but by a high degree of turbulence. There are no clear relationships between cause and effect. It may feel to the leader that there are many decisions to make and no time to think. The appropriate action here is to act to establish order, sense where stability is present and where it is absent, and then respond by driving the context towards complex or complicated.

- *Disorder* refers to those scenarios where it is unclear which of the above four contexts is predominant.

It is important to firstly emphasise that these contexts are not static—projects that start out simple can quickly find themselves in complicated, complex, or even chaotic contexts very quickly. Effective leaders must learn to adapt their approach to decision-making as contexts change over time. Equally, leaders must be mindful of the trap of mis-categorising the context in which they are operating, leading them to mismanage the situation. For example, complicated situations may appear complex to decision-makers who do not have access to all necessary information or the appropriate analytic tools.

The term 'uncertainty' appears consistently throughout the preceding discussion of complexity, which is indicative of the relationship that exists between them (and indeed, risk also). Complexity, and the underpinning interactions between the various components of the project 'system', drive risk and uncertainty on a project, as we will examine now.

Uncertainty and Risk

Projects, being future-oriented, are inherently uncertain. The fundamental problem of managing projects is dealing with uncertainty (Winch, 2010). Uncertainty is defined by Galbraith (1977) as the difference between the information required to make a decision and the information available to the decision-maker. Therefore, the greater the uncertainty around a particular task, the greater the amount of information that must be processed by decision-makers. If a task is well understood prior to performing the task, it can be robustly planned for. Where it is not understood, planning is more challenging and should allow for more information to be acquired in the future (which may lead to changes in resource allocations, schedules, and priorities; ibid.).

Winch and Maytorena (2011) take this notion forward in conveying risk and uncertainty as states of mind of the decision-maker. Risks are those future events where the likelihood of occurrence and its impact are measurable based on empirical observation, in the form of a statistical probability. Uncertainty is any future event where this is not the case, and it can take one of three forms. The authors explain the distinction between risk and the three forms of uncertainty using the taxonomy of Stephens (2003), which stemmed from a notorious speech given by then-United States Secretary of Defense, Donald Rumsfeld, in 2002:

- *Known Knowns*—often termed risks—are those future events for which the likelihood and impact can be measured using historical data and analytical techniques, upon which a decision can then be made. Whilst any decision that is made will still be a subjective judgement, it is nevertheless based on an objective calculation, based on data.
- *Known Unknowns* describe where a possible future event—an uncertainty—has been identified, but there is no reliable data upon which to base the decision-making process. In such instances, subjective probabilities are used to fill this data gap, as opposed to objective ones (as per known knowns). Given the use of subjective probabilities, known unknowns may also be particularly exposed to biases (of the sort we previously outlined in Chapter 3). Similarly, a

common pitfall here is in managing known unknowns as if they were risks: whilst the use of subjective probabilities is acceptable, they should not be regarded as if they were measured through statistical data and thus this must inform the manner in which they are managed.

- *Unknown Knowns* are uncertainties where someone is aware of the possible future event, but it has not been communicated to the decision-maker.
- *Unknown Unknowns* are uncertainties where the future event has not been identified and therefore cannot be known. The decision-maker is thus in a state of ignorance.

There is a clear link between this understanding of risk and uncertainty and our previous discussion of complexity. Put simply, complexity drives risk and uncertainty within a project. With complex projects, there are higher degrees of dynamism, and many more project elements interacting, and therefore more risk and uncertainty. Simple and complicated contexts are largely the realm of known knowns: the world is understandable, and the right answers can be determined based on facts (Winch, 2010). Complex and chaotic contexts are the realm of the unknowns, but through effective leadership and organisational tools/actions (such as those outlined in Figure 4.2), we can gain more information about the project environment and the possible future events that inhabit it. In doing so, we can move uncertainties into the realm of known knowns and potentially the project into a simple/complicated context.

Browning and Ramasesh (2015) described unknowns as coming in two forms: knowable and unknowable, and that the distinction between what is knowable on a project and what is actually known can be significant. Further, risk management—a truly pivotal facet of project management—can only prove effective on known risks (i.e. we cannot analyse things that we are not aware of). The authors outline the process of 'directed recognition' as a way of reducing complexity on projects and uncovering these 'knowable' unknowns. Directed recognition is simply a purposeful understanding of all aspects of a project (and its sub-systems) through diligent planning, analysis, scrutiny, and communication. The process involves both: (i) project design approaches, such as using checklists, analysing scenarios, scrutinising plans, mining data, and picking up on weak signals (i.e. early warning signs that significant change is underway) and (ii) behavioural approaches, such as effective communication, incentivising discovery of risks in others, and creating an 'alert culture' (whereby we collectively strive to uncover problems, rather than hide or ignore them).

Whilst such an understanding of a project should be attained during the early stages of the project lifecycle (after all, projects will only become more complex, more dynamic, and thus harder to understand), this is a process that should be emphasised and incentivised throughout the lifecycle. In so doing, further risks and issues will be uncovered and can be dealt with through the project's risk management approach, which itself should be a continuous process that is managed and maintained throughout the project lifecycle. It is this risk management process to which we now turn our attention.

Risk Management

Managing risks is an intrinsic part of project management. Risks are those things that, should they occur, will have an effect—either negative or positive (i.e. threats and opportunities)—on project outcomes. No matter how much time is invested in planning, there will still be surprises along the way. Some of these surprises could have been anticipated and planned for, such as a schedule slippage or cost overruns, whilst others, such as the economic downturn in 2020 as a result of COVID-19, are beyond imagination. We must nevertheless endeavour to expend as much effort as practical to identify risks, analyse their likelihood of occurrence and potential impact, and take action to avoid threats and seize opportunities.

It is with good reason that we address risk management as part of the broader discussion of project planning. Too often, risk management is given short shrift in the planning of projects, yet it is in the early stages of a project that the cost to fix a risk event is at its lowest, and complexity, which can cloud our perception of such events, is typically also relatively low.

Risk management should not be reactive, but proactive, whereby processes are put in place to ensure surprises are reduced and any negative consequences stemming from them are minimised (Larson and Gray, 2018). Such an approach speaks more generally of the advantages that can be reaped from 'front end loading' the project planning process (see Box 4.1)

Box 4.1 Front End Loading

Front end loading (FEL) is simply about investing the time and resources necessary to deliver the best practical project planning. As outlined by Merrow (2011), and based on research from over 21,000 projects, it is early in the project lifecycle that we have the greatest ability to influence project outcomes. The early stages are defined by flexibility, with many options still open to us, not much has been decided on, and that which has can be changed relatively easily and cheaply. Later on in the project lifecycle, expenditure increases significantly, many more decisions have been made, changes are harder to make and more costly, and there are many more interdependencies (so that one small change might lead to a lot of corrective work). The general remit of FEL is to have an executable project by the end of project planning. Merrow found significant correlations between the quality of FEL and greater predictability and effectiveness of both cost and schedule, reduced operability problems, better safety performance, and overall increased likelihood of project success. Ultimately, what is done (and not done) in planning has more bearing on project outcomes than anything else.

There are four components to the risk management process: (i) risk identification; (ii) risk assessment; (iii) risk response planning; and (iv) risk tracking and control. We will address each of these in turn in the remainder of the chapter.

Risk Identification

Risk identification begins with the generation of a list of all possible risks that could affect the project. This is typically centred around the insights of a risk management team, led by the Project Manager, who are charged with compiling such a list. Research has shown that groups make more accurate judgements about risks than individuals (Sniezek and Henry, 1989). This can involve brainstorming, so as to draw on the experience of those in the room (the process is therefore aided by the involvement of a diverse team) and lessons learned reports, so as to benefit from the wider organisational knowledge from past projects. Input from customers, sponsors, subcontractors, suppliers, and other stakeholders can also be sought. This can not only provide a valuable perspective but also attain their commitment to project success (Larson and Gray, 2018). Risks can also be identified through analysis of the WBS by scrutinising each work package in turn for potential problems that might arise. This can then be used to form a risk breakdown structure, following the same framework as the WBS.

This process should lead to the compiling of a *risk register*: a simple document that details a description of each risk (i.e. the cause) and its potential consequence(s) (i.e. the effect). It may also be desirable to include fields to categorise the risk, assign an 'owner', and record any proposed responses.

The *risk register* is a living document. As the risk management process advances, more information should be added to it. As further risks are identified later in the project lifecycle, they should equally be added to the register. As risks are managed and ultimately closed out, this too must be recorded on the register.

Risk Assessment

Not all risks are deserving of a response, and thus the next step in the process is determining which risks are significant and must be carefully managed, and which are minor and can be managed more casually. This decision is made based on a simple scenario analysis, whereby the risk management team make an assessment of: (i) the likelihood of the event occurring and (ii) the impact of the event, were it to occur. Each risk is given a score along a numerical scale (typically 1–5 or 1–10) to represent both of these dimensions. The scale does not matter as long as it is applied consistently and is easy to understand.

The likelihood score will be largely subjective, although historical data may be helpful. The impact score should be based on objective measures of key project constraints, such as cost, schedule, or other performance metrics. This will look different for each project. For example, if a component failure will incur a major increase in project cost but only a minor slip in schedule, this would be considered a high-impact risk for a project that is prioritising project cost. Conversely, on a project that is prioritising delivering on time, this would be considered a low-impact risk. What is important is that the impact is assessed in a manner congruent with the project priorities. By multiplying the likelihood score by the impact score, we get the risk's criticality.

This assessment can support the creation of a risk matrix, as shown in Figure 4.5. The example here is a 3×3 array of elements, with each element representing a different grouping of impact and likelihood values. The matrix is further divided into green, amber, and red zones, representing minor, moderate, and major risks, respectively. The matrix can be valuable in prioritising risks, with red zone risks receiving first priority, followed by amber zone risks. Green zone risks are typically considered inconsequential, unless their status changes over time. The risk register should also be updated to include this additional information (impact, likelihood, and criticality of

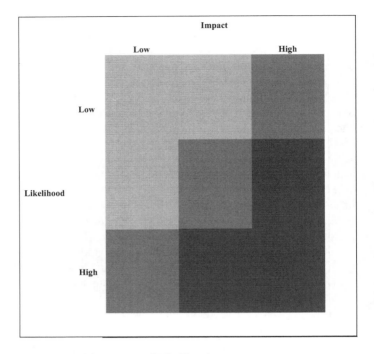

Figure 4.5 Risk Impact and Likelihood.

each risk), and this too can be used as the basis for prioritisation (e.g. what are our top ten risks by criticality?).

Risk Response Planning

Risk response planning is simply "the process of developing options and actions to enhance opportunities and reduce threats to project objectives" (PMI, 2017). There are typically four classifications of risk responses: avoid, mitigate, transfer, and accept.

Risk avoidance involves changing the project plan to eliminate the risk. Although it is not possible to avoid all risk events, some specific risks may be avoided prior to project execution. For example, moving away from an unproven technology to use a proven technology in its place, or choosing a supplier with a strong track record over the new-to-the-market supplier that offered significant price incentives. It might otherwise involve reducing the scope of the project so as to remove the problematic work component. Avoiding risk can, however, challenge the financial opportunities of a project. For example, new product development is an inherently risky endeavour, but the potential benefits can be substantial. In cases where the potential benefits are proportionate or exceed the size of the risk, the preferred approach is to mitigate the risk to an acceptable level, rather than completely avoid it (Nicholas and Steyn, 2008).

Risk mitigation can involve reducing the risk's likelihood of occurrence, its impact, or both. Focus is generally placed on reducing the likelihood of occurrence, since, if successful, this may eliminate the need for the potentially costly strategy of reducing its impact (Larson and Gray, 2018). Expertise can play a particularly significant role here. Subject matter experts could be brought in to review technical plans and cost estimates on projects, thus offering assurance of their veracity and reducing associated risks. Highly skilled personnel could be assigned the ownership of particular risks, where this suits their expertise, hence also reducing risk. Training and development can offer similar assurances (albeit with a notable time lag).

Risk transfer is a risk reduction method that passes the risk to another party. This does not change the risk but rather makes another party responsible for it (and for its consequences, should it occur). One such example is transferring the risk to a contractor in return for a financial incentive for them, built into the contract bid price. This should not be done lightly—transferring the risk does not mitigate against its impact—and careful consideration must be given to who is best placed to manage activities associated with the risk and to absorb the risk, should it occur.

Risk transfer might otherwise involve taking out an insurance policy—typically for events outside of the organisation's control, such as 'acts of God'—so that the risk is transferred to an insurance provider.

Risk acceptance may be the best option in cases where the cost of avoiding, mitigating, or transferring the risk is estimated to exceed the benefit of simply accepting it. Such a response would not be chosen for red zone risks, but there are likely to be risks on the register that are sufficiently low criticality to consider accepting them. Equally, there may be risks where nothing can be done to avoid, mitigate, or transfer the risk, regardless of their criticality, although fortunately such situations are rare (Nicholas and Steyn, 2008).

Once risk mitigation actions have been agreed, these must be updated on the risk register (along with a risk owner, if one is yet to be assigned). Best practice also dictates that 'residual risk' is also assessed at this stage. Residual risk recognises that any response put in place to manage the risk will likely not reduce its criticality to zero. The initial assessment of likelihood, impact, and criticality is often termed 'inherent risk'. The addition of residual risk—based on an assessment of the remaining likelihood, impact and criticality after implementation of the risk response—can further aid in the management and prioritisation of risk going forward.

Risk Response Tracking and Control

As noted above, the risk register is a living document and must be maintained and utilised to manage risk throughout the project lifecycle. Risk control involves executing the risk response in accordance to the agreed actions on the register, monitoring the project for weak signals of previously identified risks, as well as identifying any new risks that arise over time. This is congruent with the broader activity of tracking project progress over time. Any changes to scope, budget, and/or schedule that are enacted as a result must be managed through the project change management system (described early in this chapter).

Summary

Planning is key to project success. Too often projects jump into execution before they are ready, and a strong research base has identified the negative effects this can have on delivering on time, on budget, and to scope. In this chapter, we have focused on how to translate a set of requirements into a project scope. We then examined three elements—complexity, risk, and uncertainty—that are present in any project and can lead to project failure. Understanding these three concepts and the relationship between them, and further being able to communicate this to project personnel, can be a powerful tool for project leaders.

The next chapter will continue the exploration of the planning process, focusing on resources, schedule, and budget.

References

APM (n.d.). *Use of Product Breakdown Structures and Work Breakdown Structures* [Online]. Available at: www.apm.org.uk/resources/find-a-resource/use-of-productbreakdown-structures-and-work-breakdown-structures/ [Accessed 3 February 2024].

Browning, T.R. and Ramasesh, R.V. (2015). *Reducing unwelcome surprises in project management. MIT Sloan Management Review.* Spring 2015, pp. 53–62.

Cooper, K. and Lee, G. (2009). Managing the Dynamics of Projects and Changes at Fluor. *Proceedings of the 27th International Conference of the System Dynamics Society*, Albuquerque, New Mexico.

Coventry, T. (2015). Requirements Management—Planning for Success! Techniques to Get It Right When Planning Requirements. Paper presented at *PMI Global Congress 2015—EMEA, London.* Newtown Square, PA: Project Management Institute.

Galbraith, J.R. (1977). Organization Design: An Information Processing View, *Interfaces*, 4(3), pp. 28–36.

Haugan, G.T. (2002). *Effective Work Breakdown Structures*, Vienna, VA: Management Concepts.

IIBA (2009). *A Guide to the Business Analysis Body of Knowledge (BABOK Guide)* (Version 2.0), Toronto, Canada: International Institute of Business Analysis.

Kuster, J., Huber, E., Lippmann, R., Schmid, A., Schneider, E., Witschi, U. and Wüst, R. (2015). *Project Management Handbook*, Berlin: Springer.

Larson, E.W. and Gray, C.F. (2018). *Project Management: The Managerial Process* (7th ed.), New York: McGraw-Hill Education.

Maritato, M. (2013). Mastering the Project Requirements. Paper presented at *PMI Global Congress 2013-EMEA*, Istanbul, Turkey. Newtown Square, PA: Project Management Institute.

Merrow, E.W. (2011). *Industrial Megaprojects: Concepts, Strategies, and Practices for Success*, Hoboken, NJ: Wiley.

Merrow, E.W. and Nandurdikar, N. (2018). *Leading Complex Projects: A Data-Driven Approach to Mastering the Human Side of Project Management*, Oxford: Wiley.

Morris, P.W.G. (1994). *The Management of Projects*, London: Thomas Telford.

Nicholas, J.M. and Steyn, H. (2008). *Project Management for Business, Engineering and Technology: Principles and Practice* (3rd ed.), Oxford: Butterworth-Heinemann.

Nixon P., Harrington, M. and Parker, D. (2012). Leadership Performance Is Significant to Project Success or Failure: A Critical Analysis, *International Journal of Productivity and Performance Management*, 61(2), pp. 204–216.

PMI (2017). *A guide to the project management book of knowledge (PMBOK guide)* (6th ed.). Newtown Square, PA: Project Management Institute.

PMI (2021). *A Guide to the Project Management Body of Knowledge (PMBOK Guide)* (7th ed.), Newtown Square, PA: Project Management Institute.

PMI (2023). *Process Groups: A Practice Guide*, Newtown Square, PA: Project Management Institute.

Sniezek, J.A. and Henry, R.A. (1989). Accuracy and Confidence in Group Judgment, *Organizational Behavior and Human Decision Processes*, 43(1), pp. 1–28.

Snowden, D.J. and Boone, M.E. (2007). A Leader's Framework for Decision Making, *Harvard Business Review*, November, pp. 68–76.

Standish Group (2004). *CHAOS Report 2004*, West Yarmouth, MA: Standish Group International.

Stephens, P. (2003). The Unwitting Wisdom of Rumsfeld's Unknowns, *Financial Times*, December 12, 9.

Turner, J.R. and Müller, R. (2005). The Project Manager's Leadership Style as a Success Factor on Projects: A Literature Review, *Project Management Journal*, 36(2), pp. 49–61.

Wells, K. and Kloppenborg, T. (2015). *Project Management Essentials*, New York: Business Expert Press.

Winch, G.M. (2010). *Managing Construction Projects* (2nd ed.), Singapore: Blackwell Publishing.

Winch, G.M. and Maytorena, E. (2011). Managing Risk and Uncertainty on Projects: A Cognitive Approach. In: Morris, P.W.G., Pinto, J. and Söderlund, J. (eds.), *The Oxford Handbook of Project Management*, Oxford: Oxford University Press. pp. 345–364.

Yang, L.R., Huang, C.F. and Wu, K.S. (2011). The Association Among Project Manager's Leadership Style, Teamwork and Project Success, *International Journal of Project Management*, 29(3), pp. 258–267.

5 Project Planning

Schedule, Resources, and Budget

Introduction

This second of three chapters examining the planning process is focused on how to plan the timing of activities, the allocation of resources, and the financial expenditure on a project. Almost all projects must operate within constraints of time, resources, and money, and we examine the various plans that can be put in place to ensure the project remains viable and achievable against these constraints. This includes coordinating people resources through an organisational breakdown structure, determining the sequence of work activities with a network diagram, building a robust schedule (or Gantt chart), and developing a reliable budget.

Resources

In project management, resources refer to the people, equipment, materials, tools, facilities, and other assets required to carry out project activities and achieve project objectives. Resource management, then, involves identifying, acquiring, allocating, and optimising resources throughout the project lifecycle.

This starts with first estimating the types and quantities of resources required to perform each activity within the work breakdown structure (WBS). However, the task is certainly complicated on most projects by the fact that the quantities of resources needed to perform project activities are limited and in

DOI: 10.4324/9781003057246-5

competition with the organisation's other projects. Therefore, resources can constrain a project's progress and, if poorly managed, can lead to delays. We must consider these constraints during project planning because taking corrective action during execution can prove extremely difficult and costly.

It is important to first make a distinction between two types of constraints on projects. *Technical Constraints* arise because one activity (the successor) requires the output from another (the predecessor) before work can commence. For example, if constructing a house, the foundations must be poured before the exterior walls can be constructed, after which the roof can be constructed (see Figure 5.1). These three activities must occur in sequence: the successor cannot start until the predecessor activity has been completed.

Resource Constraints, on the other hand, involve limitations or restrictions related to the availability, quantity, or capacity of resources. Where activities are executed in parallel (unlike those in Figure 5.1, which are in a serial relationship), resource constraints may lead to conflicts. Another example is shown in Figure 5.2, this time illustrating the difference between various degrees of resource constraint on a house renovation project.

In example (c), there are no technical constraints in place: each activity can be performed in parallel. However, (a) and (b) demonstrate the potential for resource constraints to impact the progress made on a project. If, for the example above, it takes one painter one day to paint a room, project (c) will be complete in one day, whereas project (a) would take three days. Hence, as with technical constraints, resource constraints can significantly impact the scheduling and total duration of a project and must

Figure 5.1 Technical Constraints of a House Build.

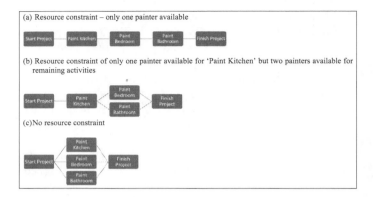

Figure 5.2 Resource Constraints of a House Renovation.

be carefully considered and planned for: a failure to do so may gravely impact project success.

Resource Requirements

We start by estimating for each type of resource (people, facilities, materials, equipment, etc.) the quantity and specification required to execute each activity on the WBS. For some projects, it will not be possible to determine an accurate picture of the resource requirements for the entire duration of the project (i.e. those projects that have a very long duration, or otherwise a high degree of uncertainty). In such cases, detailed resource requirements should be developed over a suitable timeline, with more of an overview approach taken for the later stages of the project.

For most projects, many of the activities are not new to the organisation and will have been performed on previous projects. That historical context—and, ideally, historical data—can provide a very useful basis for establishing resource requirements on the current project.

People Resources

People are the most difficult type of resource to plan since it calls for a greater level of detail to be gathered than other forms of resources (Wysocki, 2019). We must first determine the human resources we need to perform the project activities, including their skills, knowledge, accreditations, and professional certifications. You do not identify the individual but rather the person specification that you need. Roles and responsibilities and lines of authority should also be defined at this stage. A plan should also be established for how to acquire, train, develop, retain, and motivate human resources during their time on the project.

Once there is a good level of detail around the resource requirements of the project with regards to personnel, there are two tools of note that can aid in graphically conveying this information. The first is the organisational breakdown structure (OBS; see Figure 5.3). The OBS looks a lot like a PBS or WBS but in this case represents all the people on the project, the team to which they are assigned, and their lines of authority (you may know this otherwise as an 'Organisational Chart', an 'Org. Chart', or an 'Organogram').

The OBS will continue to evolve over the life of the project and may later include the names of the individuals, rather than just the roles.

With both the work activities and the project team structure now defined, we can specify what exactly each project member will be responsible for. A responsibility assignment matrix (RAM) exists for this very purpose: to illustrate the project activities and how project personnel are assigned to various responsibilities for each. One such model is a RACI chart, which assigns the following responsibilities:

- *Responsible (R):* the person who is responsible for completing the task or activity. There must be at least one person responsible for each activity (although there may be more than one person with this responsibility).

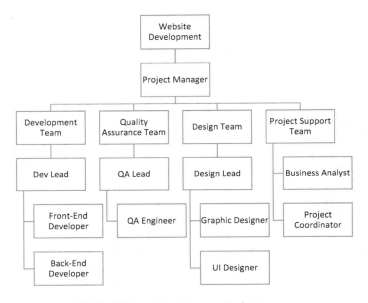

Figure 5.3 OBS for Website Development Project.

- *Accountable (A):* the person who 'owns' the activity and is ultimately responsible for ensuring the work is completed satisfactorily. There should only be one person assigned this responsibility for each activity, so as to avoid confusion.
- *Consulted (C):* an individual whose expertise or input is sought during the execution of the task or activity. Requires two-way communication with those performing the activity.
- *Informed (I):* an individual who should be kept aware of the progress and outcome of the task or activity. They are not directly involved in the execution of the activity, and this therefore requires only one-way communication.

An example is show in Figure 5.4.

A RACI carries some notable advantages. First, it streamlines communication and decision-making by only

Task	Project Manager	Dev Lead	FE Developer	BE Developer	QA Lead	QA Engineer	Design Lead	Graphic Designer	UI Designer	Business Analyst	Project Coordinator
Define project requirements	A/R	R	C	C	R	C	R	I	I	R	C
Conduct user research	C	C	-	-	C	C	C	-	-	A/R	C
Develop front-end code	C	A	R	-	C	C	-	-	-	-	-
Develop back-end code	C	A	-	R	C	C	-	-	-	-	-
Perform quality assurance testing	C	C	C	C	A	R	-	-	-	-	-
Design and implement database	C	A	-	R	-	-	-	-	-	-	-
Conduct user acceptance testing	C	C	C	C	A	R	-	-	-	-	-
Prepare project documentation	A/R	C	C	C	C	C	C	-	-	R	C
Deployment and release	C	A	R	R	C	C	-	-	-	-	-

Figure 5.4 RACI for Website Development Project.

involving the right people at the right time in an activity. The important distinction between the *consulted* and *informed* responsibilities illustrates this. It encourages delegation and avoids overloading individuals (most commonly, the Project Manager) and working in silos. The use of colour can quickly identify those that might be carrying too much responsibility across the project's work activities. Finally, it also sets clear expectations at this early stage around responsibilities and communication. Everyone can understand how they will be involved in the project, which avoids confusion later on when the work is executed.

There is now the challenge of identifying potential personnel to work on the project. The Project Manager must identify suitable candidates, in consideration of: their work history, range of responsibilities, professional discipline (e.g. qualifications, professional certifications, etc.), skill level and experience, their physical location (and willingness to relocate or travel), and their pay expectations and current contract (Kloppenborg et al., 2019). With this information, the Project Manager can compare the available personnel with the resource requirements to highlight any gaps with regards to either skill or quantity of personnel. Any gaps can be addressed by the Project Manager with support from the sponsor and the wider organisation.

Timing is also critical to this process: when to bring people on board. We must be aware, of course, of the cost associated with bringing each new member into the project. However, failure to bring an important resource on board may delay the project schedule. The answer lies in bringing key members on board as early as possible. Such people are typically highly experienced and capable, and hence, can be involved in the planning of the project, its early progress, and establishing an effective project culture (Kloppenborg et al., 2019).

Scheduling

Scheduling involves the sequencing of work activities so that the work is completed in the optimal time. It builds upon the work already done in developing a set of activities in the WBS. Just as the project scope serves as a baseline for the work to be done, the schedule, once agreed by the Project Sponsor, will serve as a baseline for when it will be done. The schedule is a crucial guiding document for the project, as well as an important mechanism by which to measure project progress and performance.

An effective project schedule should consider several possible limitations, as outlined by Wells and Kloppenborg (2015), and the preceding section of this chapter has already discussed these in part. First, the technical constraints—the logical order in which some, if not all, of the activities can be performed—must be planned for. This is discussed further in the subsequent sub-section. Secondly, we know that projects operate under an environment of constrained resources, and thus we must schedule activities in a manner that ensures individual personnel are not overloaded and resources are available when we need them. Finally, some project schedules are constrained financially and this too must be planned for, as will be addressed later in this chapter.

Sequencing Work Activities

Our starting point is the WBS. Once the work activities have been defined, as in the manner of the WBS, they can be sequenced. The WBS already provides groupings of activities (which may indicate work performed by different people/teams), but we are also looking for both a logical order in which to perform these activities and the dependencies between them: which activities cannot be performed until after certain other activities have been completed (taking into account the technical constraints and resource constraints as discussed above).

It can be useful to develop a network diagram to support this process. Activities from the WBS are represented as boxes or 'nodes', connected in accordance with the logical sequence in which they should be performed, how many activities can logically be performed at the same time, and the resource constraints under which the project is operating.

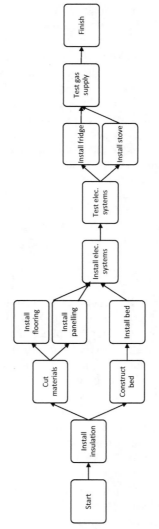

Figure 5.5 Network Diagram (Authors' Own).

An example for the campervan conversion project described in Chapter 4 is shown in Figure 5.5. Please note, the activities from the WBS have been simplified here so that the example is legible. In practice, all lowest-level activities from the WBS must be included in the network diagram. Any omissions could lead to inaccuracies around schedule duration, estimated costs, and resource availability.

The example shows that some activities can be performed concurrently but many cannot: dependencies exist which dictate that the previous activity is completed before the next one can commence in order to deliver the work package. It should be noted that whilst this finish-to-start relationship is most common, other relationships can be shown with the network diagram, such as how far along one activity must be before another can start, or where an activity must be completed x number of days before the next can start (such relationships are easily programmable in project scheduling software; Kloppenborg, 2009).

This starts to build a picture of the possible sequencing of activities, but we need further information in order to develop a detailed schedule. Providing an estimate of the duration of each activity will allow us to determine the *critical path* through the sequence. The critical path is simply the longest path through the project activities from start to finish. By tallying the durations of all activities on the critical path, we can identify the shortest possible duration for the project. Presuming we know the intended start date of the project, we will therefore also now know the earliest end date.

An example from the same campervan project is shown in Figure 5.6, with the critical path highlighted. We now know the total duration for the project is 6.5 days.

The critical path also highlights those activities that are most important to the project's timely delivery and thus should be the focus of more of the Project Manager's attention: any delay to the activities on the critical path will delay the project as a whole. Where two or more paths are the equally longest paths through the network, those are your critical *paths*. All other

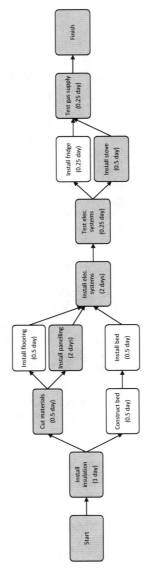

Figure 5.6 Network Diagram with Critical Path (Authors' Own).

paths have some permissible delay: they can lose *some* time without it impacting the final delivery of the project. This permissible delay is called 'float' or 'slack'.

It is possible to experiment at this early stage by testing the impact of changes on the diagram with 'what-if' questions, such as:

- Will it impact the project duration if we start activity *x* late?
- Does starting activity *x* early change the work package's delivery date?
- Which tasks should we consider to speed up delivery?
- Is there a benefit to assigning extra resource to activity *x*?
- If resources for activity *x* are further constrained, what is the impact?

These what-if scenarios may become reality in project execution, whereby if critical activities are completed earlier than planned and/or others suffer unexpected delays, the critical path may change. The Project Manager must therefore be careful to manage the system of activities as a whole and not focus solely on the critical path (Maylor and Turner, 2022).

Estimating Duration

Estimating is a crucial part of project planning and can begin once activities have been defined and sequenced. However, they are particularly exposed to bias and strategic misrepresentation (as discussed in Chapter 3). As Maylor and Turner (2022) remind us, "estimates, unless based on good data (i.e. how long this task normally takes), are better termed 'guesses'". Further, without reliable estimates, all other aspects of time and cost management are undermined.

The project will later rely on the quality of these estimates to deliver the project on time (and, similarly, with regards to cost, on budget—discussed later in this chapter). However, there are several factors related to the uniqueness of a project that will strongly influence the accuracy of estimates (Larson and Gray, 2018):

- *Planning Horizon:* estimates for current events are typically close to 100% accurate but those further ahead in the future are less reliable. The accuracy of estimates should improve as you move through the project lifecycle and there is more information available. For this reason, estimating should be seen as an iterative and ongoing process through the project's life.
- *Complexity:* as per the discussion in Chapter 4, the greater the complexity in a project (be that developing a new technology, working with a wide range of stakeholders, or managing a long duration project), the greater the uncertainty. This uncertainty also finds its way into our estimates.
- *Skills-base:* estimating is complex, and like anything complex, it takes time and skills to produce. The skill level of those involved—both their 'estimating skills' and their professional skills in the underlying discipline—will affect the accuracy of the estimate.
- *Culture:* organisations vary in the importance they place on accuracy in the estimating process. Some organisations champion a focus on accuracy in estimates as the foundation for project success. Others will push the idea that we cannot predict the future and hence detailed estimating is not worth the time and effort it requires. Culture influences every facet of project management, and estimating is no exception.

Box 5.1 illustrates one possible technique for enhancing the robustness of planning estimates.

As with the assessment of resource requirements, estimating duration should rely on expertise and previous experience, wherever available. However, this comes with some challenges, as discussed by Wysocki (2019). One person might be optimistic and another pessimistic but you will not know unless you have evidence of one or the other.

Box 5.1 Calculating the Expected Time for an Activity Duration Using Three-Point Estimating

Three-point estimating can be used to estimate the duration of an activity (particularly where there is uncertainty about the duration) by calculating a weighted average (a beta distribution) of optimistic, pessimistic, and most likely estimates, weighing the most likely estimate more strongly than the pessimistic and optimistic estimates.

Given:
t_o = the most optimistic time estimate for the activity
t_m = the most likely time estimate for the activity
t_p = the most pessimistic time estimate for the activity

t_e = the expected time for the activity, is

$$t_e = \frac{t_o + 4t_m + t_p}{6}$$

It is important to involve the person who will be responsible for estimating the duration and resources required, but this too can be problematic. That person might overestimate the time and resources required to enhance their chances of meeting their deadlines. Some team members may be overly optimistic about how quickly they can complete a certain activity (often because they do not foresee time constraints such as rework, sickness, annual leave, training, and learning curves).

These issues can be partially addressed by involving multiple people, including subject matter experts, in an estimate. Discussion of differences between estimates from individuals can lead to consensus and eliminate extreme errors (Larson and Gray, 2018). Data is also an invaluable input. Historical records from past projects may include not only previous estimates for similar activities but ideally also the actual duration it took to complete that activity. Records from multiple previous projects can be combined to arrive at an average duration.

Some activities will be much shorter than others, but to avoid confusion and errors, the same unit of time should be used for all activities. This is typically either weeks, workdays, or hours. It is also best practice to record any assumptions upon which your estimates were based, since a change to one of these assumptions could change the estimate (Kloppenborg et al., 2019). The estimates for the time for the work to be done must include any associated waiting time.

Wysocki (2019) emphasises that no matter how long is spent estimating a task, the estimated duration remains a random variable, and outlines several factors that can later impact actual duration once the task is executed:

- *Varying skill levels:* higher or lower-skilled personnel than planned may be assigned to the activity, leading the actual duration to vary from the planned duration. Similarly, the learning curve and rate of improvement on new tasks will be more pronounced for some workers than others.
- *Unexpected events:* anything from a random act of nature, to supplier delays, to a materials shortage can occur (amongst many other things), leading to the actual duration extending beyond the estimate.
- *Efficiency:* you cannot control the frequency or timing of interruptions, but when they do occur, they impact the productivity of personnel.
- *Mistakes and misunderstandings:* inaccuracy or misconstruction of work instructions can arise on projects, which may lead to rework or scrapping incomplete work;
- *Common cause variation:* the actual duration will vary simply because duration is a random variable. The process of estimating has a natural variation that we cannot control for and must be accepted.

Any changes impacting the schedule—be they initiated by the customer, project team, or from unanticipated occurrences—and their resulting corrective actions should lead us to update the project schedule and determine whether the critical path has now changed.

Reducing the Duration

In almost every case, the initial project estimates will result in a forecasted completion date later than the required completion date (Wysocki, 2019). Later, in the Executing stage, we might find that we are several weeks behind schedule, or the customer may offer a significant financial incentive if we can bring the project in a month ahead of schedule. In such cases, we must look for ways to reduce the duration of the project.

Naturally, we can look first at the critical path and ways in which it could be shortened. This might include (Larson and Gray, 2018; Kloppenborg, 2019):

- Reducing the project scope and/or quality: there may be nice-to-have features that can be sacrificed once their schedule impact is understood. This will typically require permission from the sponsor and/or customer.
- Scheduling activities that are normally in sequence to run in parallel (this is often termed *fast tracking*), or partially overlapping sequential activities. This will often have a risk impact, since the project will become more difficult to manage with more activities taking place at the same time.
- Shortening activities by assigning more resources or increasing the number of work hours per day or workdays per week (often termed *crashing*). This will have a cost impact (the cost of labour) and may also affect the productivity and efficiency of work. A similar alternative is to outsource elements of project work to a third party.

We can see the Project Management Triangle (refer to Chapter 1) in the description above. When trying to reduce the duration, the Project Manager must decide which of scope/quality, risk, or cost/productivity they are willing to sacrifice in return for a quicker delivery.

Building a Schedule

The logic from sequencing the activities, as dictated by the network diagram, can now be used to further outline when the activities will be carried out. The most common schedule technique for this is a simple bar chart, called a 'Gantt chart'. Each activity has its own row along a vertical scale (which can be grouped by work packages), accompanied by a horizontal scale representing time (in hours, days, weeks, or months, as appropriate). The starting and completion times of activities and whole work packages are indicated by coloured bars. A simple example, based on the network diagram in Figure 5.6, is shown in Figure 5.7. It is possible to add further detail to the Gantt chart, such as dependencies between activities (noted with arrows, as per the network diagram), and the float time of individual activities (typically noted as lines running horizontally ahead of the bar to the latest possible finish time).

The utility of the Gantt chart is its ability to communicate the plan. Whilst we need the logic of the network diagram to create the plan, this is not the best way to communicate it to the project team. A Gantt chart is generally simple to construct (and a module of any project management software solution) and easy to understand.

The main weakness of Gantt charts is that they are often viewed as a picture of *what will happen*, rather than *what we would like to happen* (Maylor and Turner, 2022). It is important to remember the uncertainty present in any project plan. We have discussed above the possible causes of such uncertainty, and project managers must be mindful of this and act accordingly. Developing a schedule (or resource plan or budget)

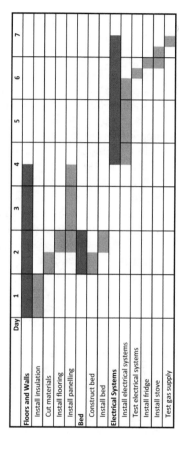

Figure 5.7 Gantt Chart (Authors' Own).

should be viewed as an iterative process, with project managers striving to improve and update plans as more information becomes available, project deliverables are better understood, and work is completed through the lifecycle.

Budgeting

At this stage, we know the resources required to deliver the work and when that work will take place. This is the information needed to then establish the total cost of the project and develop a budget. During Project Initiating, high-level estimates of costs are developed to support the project selection and chartering processes (discussed in Chapter 3). Now, the detailed planning must start around cost in the form of a budget, which may be used later to verify once again that the project is still viable and achievable prior to Executing.

As with resource requirements and the schedule, the budget is based on estimates. One of the reasons that so many projects go over budget is that people believe they have delivered a perfect estimate first time that is then set in stone (Wysocki, 2019). The same uncertainty in our schedule will also be present in our budget. The accuracy of cost estimates will be equally challenged by the constraints described above in discussing scheduling (Larson and Gray, 2018): planning horizon, project complexity, skills-base, culture, bias, and strategic misrepresentation. By extension, much of the best practice for avoiding some of these pitfalls also applies here. Where possible, organisations should utilise previous similar projects as a reference point for realistic costs. However, caution must be taken to capture the unique characteristics of the current project in the estimating figures. Subject matter experts can similarly play an important role here in sense-checking these figures.

As we discussed with the schedule above, there may be pressure to reduce the costs of the project, a phenomenon Merrow (2011) calls "we need to shave 20 percent off that number!"—again, the Project Management Triangle reminds us that the cost of a project is inextricably linked to its scope, and if both have been estimated realistically, changing the cost of a project without changing its scope is unwise (ibid).

Organisations should develop a standard costing database for common resources to be used across their projects. A Project Manager can take this database and develop a table for calculating the cost by multiplying the quantity of resource by the unit cost and/or work hours for which it will be required. Any one-time or fixed costs can also be added. The table can group costs by work package and/or deliverable. This table is sometimes referred to as a *cost breakdown structure*.

Many organisations utilise a 'contingency reserve' to address the uncertainty that is present in the budget. This might be for risks that have been identified but may not come to pass, for example. This reserve is included in the budget and is held in reserve until/unless needed.

The costing data can be combined with the schedule data so that the budget not only outlines how much money will be required to fund the project but also *when* it will be needed (i.e. the project's cash flow). Cash flow is a significant challenge for organisations who will often have multiple projects in different stages of development at any one time. A failure to plan for cash flow can lead to significant delays or even the cancellation of the project. Once established, actual cash flow can be tracked against what was planned.

Consolidating Resources, Schedule, and Budget

So far, this chapter has demonstrated the ways in which the planning of resources, scheduling, and budgeting are inherently linked. Weaknesses in one will reflect directly in the others. Many projects ultimately fail due to these critical processes being given short shrift, with imprecise or unreliable estimates proving harmful during execution with regards to the project's cost performance, schedule performance, issues with operability and/or safety, and overall chances of success (as per our brief discussion of front end loading in Chapter 4; Merrow, 2011).

In Chapter 4, we discussed the process by which the scope is 'baselined' and thereafter controlled through the change management process. The same must take place with regards to the plans for schedule, budget, and resources. The plan for these elements must be agreed with the stakeholders and consequently the team must be committed to achieving the plan. Once baselined, if anyone requests a change to the schedule, the budget, or the resources, it must be made through the change management process, with the change assessed for its impact and, if approved, the plan changed accordingly.

Summary

This chapter has expanded on the focus on planning in the preceding chapter. We have seen how the plan around *what* work will take place is advanced in consideration of both technical and resource constraints into a picture of *how* it will take place: the network diagram. The delivery of such work requires resources, the availability of which can significantly impact the scheduling and total duration of a project. Our most important resources are people, and we have outlined multiple techniques and considerations in the organising and planning of these resources. We have outlined how the network diagram can be developed further into the schedule in the form of the Gantt chart, which is used to communicate the plan. This has included a discussion of how to compress the schedule, if desired. We have also discussed the process of developing a budget. Throughout this chapter, we have emphasised the importance of accurate and reliable estimates, whether these are for cost, time, or resources, along with, importantly, some common pitfalls to avoid and best practices to follow.

The next chapter will complete our work on the planning process with an examination of the planning of stakeholder engagement and communication.

References

Kloppenborg, T. (2009). *Project Management: A Contemporary Approach*, Mason, OH: South-Western Cengage Learning.

Kloppenborg, T., Anantatmula, V. and Wells, K. (2019). *Contemporary Project Management* (4th ed.), Boston, MA: Cengage.

Larson, E.W. and Gray, C.F. (2018). *Project Management: The Managerial Process* (7th ed.), New York: McGraw-Hill Education.

Maylor, H. and Turner, N. (2022). *Project Management* (5th ed.), Harlow: Pearson.

Merrow, E.W. (2011). *Industrial Megaprojects: Concepts, Strategies, and Practices for Success*, Hoboken, NJ: Wiley.

Wells, K. and Kloppenborg, T. (2015). *Project Management Essentials*, New York, NY: Business Expert Press.

Wysocki, R.K. (2019). *Effective Project Management: Traditional, Agile, Extreme, Hybrid* (8th ed.), Indianapolis, IN: Wiley.

6   Project Planning

Stakeholder and Communication
Management

Introduction

This chapter addresses the challenge of stakeholder and communication management. Quite simply, stakeholders can make or break a project, and therefore, engagement with stakeholders must be carefully planned and managed. We discuss how to identify stakeholders, how to analyse them through a *power-interest matrix*, and how to then use this insight to build a plan around their management. Importantly, we also discuss how to build relationships and engage meaningfully and effectively with stakeholders. Good communication is at the heart of stakeholder management, and we therefore also discuss effective communication management towards the end of the chapter.

Stakeholder Management

A project stakeholder is "an individual, group, or organisation who may affect, be affected by, or perceive itself to be affected by a decision, activity, or outcome of a project" (Miller and Oliver, 2015). Stakeholders will be present on every project, regardless of its size, but we know from our discussion of shaping complexity (refer to Chapter 4) that the larger the project, generally the greater the number of stakeholders (and hence greater the socio-political complexity). This includes (Kloppenborg et al., 2019):

DOI: 10.4324/9781003057246-6

- People who work on the project.
- Companies providing resources for the project.
- Individuals whose routines are disrupted by the project.
- Organisations monitoring regulations, laws, standards, etc. at local, regional, and national levels.

Importantly, this includes both those internal and external to the project organisation. Internal stakeholders will include: project owner(s), senior leaders, Project Sponsor(s), the Project Manager, the project team, functional managers and teams, shareholders, and the internal customer and users (on internal projects). Despite their necessary involvement in projects, many internal stakeholders know very little about how projects are managed and often have little incentive to find out more or to cooperate (Merrow and Nandurdikar, 2018).

External stakeholders may include suppliers, partners, contractors, creditors, government agencies, neighbours and community groups, unions, the client/customer/users, and the media.

Project managers are often drawn to the measures of success around scope, time, cost, and quality (i.e. the Project Management Triangle; Figure 1.1). However, in the longer-term, projects will be judged a success or failure more on the impact the project has made on its stakeholders. For example, if we consider the Leaning Tower of Pisa, that project can be viewed as a failure if we consider certain stakeholders (e.g. the original designers and builders) or an unplanned success (e.g. for the local and national tourist trade). This example illustrates the diversity in perceptions that might exist around a project (both during and after its lifecycle). It is for this reason that we must plan for and manage stakeholders carefully.

A particularly insightful group of executive learners recently reflected that "project problems are people problems". Simply, a huge part of a Project Manager's job is how to manage, but also how to utilise, people. Just as with the project's own team, stakeholders too should be regarded as a valuable resource. We must first understand who they are and what they want, later focusing on how to prioritise and manage them.

Identifying Stakeholders

As already discussed, stakeholders will include a wide range of individuals, groups, and organisations, both internal and external to the project organisation. The first step in managing stakeholders lies in compiling a complete account of who they are. Bourne (2015) offers a useful framework for this, which goes beyond the internal/external dichotomy to encourage the consideration of stakeholders that exist:

- Upwards, such as senior leaders of the organisation, sponsors, government bodies, regulators, etc., to maintain organisational commitment.
- Outwards, such as customers, end users, partners, creditors, unions, suppliers, contractors, functional managers/team members, shareholders, government, and 'the public'.
- Sidewards: peers to the Project Manager, communities of practice, and competitors.
- Downwards: members of the project team.

Each of these stakeholder groups will bring different expertise, expectations, standards, and agendas to the project (Larson and Gray, 2018).

Project managers and their teams (often in consultation with the Project Sponsor) can work collectively to consider all stakeholders for their project across these dimensions. The guiding question can be "who may affect, be affected by, or perceive themselves/itself to be affected by a decision, activity, or outcome of a project" (as per Miller and Oliver, 2015). It is important to carefully consider all stakeholders of the project, since any unidentified stakeholder may represent a missed opportunity to gain the support of a valuable ally, or to prevent the later disruption of a negative stakeholder. Further, the support of one stakeholder may affect the Project Manager's ability to manage other stakeholders: for example, the cooperation of functional managers may be contingent on the perception of strong support for the project from the organisation's senior leaders (Larson and Gray, 2018).

Once an exhaustive list of stakeholders has been generated, it can be analysed.

Analysing Stakeholders

We analyse stakeholders so that we can prioritise them. Not all stakeholders are deserving of management efforts, nor do project managers have the time or resources to manage every stakeholder (Eskerod and Jepsen, 2013). We need a clear indication of who is vital to the success of the project: our 'key stakeholders' to manage closely. Beyond key stakeholders, the ranking by importance of all other stakeholders is useful when faced with competing demands from different stakeholders whose expectations cannot be met or may even be in conflict (Wells and Kloppenborg, 2015).

Stakeholders can be analysed based on their level of one or more criteria, such as:

- Power to affect the project's outcome.
- Interest in the project process and/or the outcome.
- Support—their likelihood to support the project.
- Urgency—time sensitivity or the need for immediate attention.
- Legitimacy—how much of a 'right' they have to participate, and how appropriate their involvement is.
- Influence over the project and its other stakeholders.

There are several prescribed techniques that use a combination of these criteria, such as the salience model (which uses power, legitimacy, and urgency; Mitchell et al., 1997) and the power-interest matrix (Eden and Ackermann, 1998). We will focus on the latter here, but regardless of which technique or which combination of criteria is chosen, the process looks the same. Each stakeholder is rated for each criterion: either high, medium, or low, or similarly a score of 1–3 (with 3 representing the highest priority). With two or three criteria, this can be represented graphically on a 'stakeholder map', an example of which for power and interest is shown in Figure 6.1. Alternatively, a table can be created of each criterion and each stakeholder and their respective scores, much like a risk register. Those stakeholders with the highest score on the register, or highest position on the stakeholder map, will be the project's key stakeholders.

We can see from Figure 6.1 that there are three distinct categories within the power-interest matrix beyond that of the high priority/key stakeholders. An advantage of this approach is that the authors prescribe specific actions for how to communicate with, influence, and manage stakeholders based on their

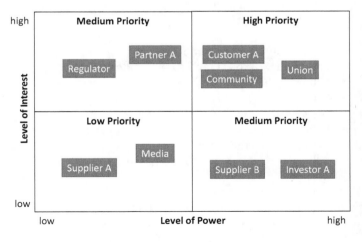

Figure 6.1 Example Power-Interest Matrix.

location on the stakeholder map, rather than focusing solely on the key stakeholders (Ackermann and Eden, 2011):

- Low power and low interest: these are the *Crowd* stakeholders, not so much stakeholders as could-be stakeholders. At present, these stakeholders are unlikely to be worth management effort and resources. However, there interest and/or power could increase, and as such, we should monitor this over time.
- Low power and high interest: known as *Subjects*. There are several options here, depending on whether the stakeholder is in support of or against the project (or agnostic/ undecided). With a group of positively disposed Subjects, there is an opportunity to build a coalition to increase their collective power. However, a negative stakeholder in this position is a potential threat, and we could look to neutralise this by changing their attitude towards the project through communication.
- High power and low interest: *Context Setters* are named as such for their ability to influence the overall future context. A positive stakeholder here represents an opportunity to raise their awareness of the project, and thus their interest, making them a valuable ally. This may be achieved by inviting their contribution or requesting their help on the project, possibly even offering them a formal role on the project. Conversely, a negative Context Setter can be addressed by attempting to reduce their power base or looking for potential substitutes.
- High power and high interest: finally, the *Players* are those who require sustained management attention. A positive stakeholder here can be very powerful, but equally a negative Player can create a lot of problems for a project. Just as with subjects and context setters, the management of Players relies on effective communication and relationship building.

The project team should next select those stakeholders who will be the focus of planning and management effort, based on this enhanced understanding from the analysis process. As discussed earlier, the project team will need to pay particular attention to the key stakeholders. However, a more informed approach would ensure that the interests of all stakeholders—including the low priority ones—are at least considered (Eskerod et al., 2015). Once this selection has been made, a plan can be developed.

Stakeholder Planning

Once the assessment of stakeholders' priority, disposition, and expectations from the project have been assessed, we are now in a position to develop a stakeholder management plan. The preceding analysis has created a picture of how the world is, but we have agency here and can consider the actions that can be taken to foster more fruitful stakeholder relationships and minimise issues. The plan will often include: each stakeholder selected for management effort; what their goals, interests, and/ or expectations from the project are; the engagement actions and/or strategy that will be put in place; and, importantly, who within the project team will be responsible for executing these actions, and a deadline by which to do so. An example template is shown in Figure 6.2.

Stakeholder (who they are)	Goals/ Interests/ Expectations (what they want)	Management Strategy/Actions (how to manage)	Responsibility/ Timeline (who will manage and when)

Figure 6.2 Example Stakeholder Management Plan Template.

As with all project plans, the stakeholder plan must remain a living document through the life of the project. A significant misstep for many projects—in addition to leaving this process too late, perhaps even until in project execution—is to not regularly review the stakeholder plan. The stakeholder landscape is dynamic: a stakeholder's level of interest or power (or any of the other noted criteria above) can change over time. A further level of dynamism stems from the fact that stakeholders can also influence and change one another's level of power and interest or their perception of the project; of course, project managers can also try to use this to their advantage through engagement actions. For these reasons, it must be regularly reviewed.

For someone new to the process, the generation of effective engagement actions may appear challenging, but at its heart is relationship building and communication. We will look at each of these further in the remainder of this chapter.

Stakeholder Relationships and Engagement

The development of strong working relationships with key stakeholders is a cornerstone of effective project management. An advantage of starting the stakeholder process here, in Planning, is that strong stakeholder relationships are at their most effectual in Executing. The most significant problems on projects are typically entailed in Executing, and it is in Executing that stakeholders have the greatest scope to disrupt or positively support the project. We know too how important strong relationships and open communication with key stakeholders, and particularly the customer/end user, are to the scoping process, the lack of which remains a significant pitfall of many projects (discussed in Chapter 4).

It is often said that it is important to build stakeholder relationships before you will need them (the same is equally true in the case of relationships amongst the project team, and particularly between the Project Manager and their team). We know from our discussion of complexity and uncertainty (refer to Chapter 4) that project managers must be proactive in deepening their understanding of all aspects of the project. In this case, we need to get to know our stakeholders better as people—what motivates them, what concerns them, etc.—and focus on building relationships on principles of trust, credibility, and open communication. People are naturally more inclined to be cooperative with those with whom they have personal relationships. As Merrow and Nandurdikar (2018) conclude, "the test of leadership is getting people who don't have to agree to follow willingly and even enthusiastically".

Traditional notions of 'what a leader is' did not ascribe much value to these competencies. However, increasing focus has been placed recently on the ability of leaders to communicate effectively and build relationships with their team and their stakeholders. Effective communication requires both communicating with, but also actively listening to, your stakeholders. A leader must know when to listen, when to advocate, when to inquire, when to negotiate, when to persuade, when to influence, when to coach, and when to resolve issues/conflict. Ancona et al. (2007) offer the following guidance to leaders in building relationships:

1 Spend time trying to understand others' perspectives, listening with an open mind and without judgement.
2 Encourage others to voice their opinions. What do they care about? How do they interpret what's going on? Why?
3 Before expressing your ideas, try to anticipate how others will react to them and how you might best explain them.
4 When expressing your ideas, don't just give a bottom line; explain your reasoning process.
5 Assess the strengths of your current relationships: How well do you relate to others when receiving advice? When giving advice? When thinking through difficult problems? When asking for help?

At the core of this is *emotional intelligence*. Merrow and Nandurdikar (2018), building on the work of Goleman (2004), affirm the significance of emotional intelligence to effective project leadership. Emotional intelligence, as described by the former, consists of

- How well one reads other's emotions.
- How well one reads one's own emotions.
- How effectively one regulates emotions.
- Social skills.
- The ability to use emotions instrumentally.
- Optimism.

Merrow and Nandurdikar's comprehensive study finds that strengths in these areas, combined with the leader's personality—specifically, being open (to views and opinions of others, and to different ways of approaching a problem), emotionally stable, and highly conscientious—translate directly into the most important leadership tasks for a project leader: working with others, team management, communication, and stakeholder management. Goleman (2004) emphasises that this is different from being generally intelligent, which is why many smart people fail as leaders.

Whilst we have emphasised the importance of planning stakeholder engagement and building relationships early in the project's life, this is an activity that will continue until the last days of the project. In fact, many project managers continue to nurture their relationships after project completion to maintain good will with stakeholders and improve the chances of winning further project work and securing valuable people resources in the future (Kloppenborg et al., 2019).

Given that communication is at the heart of stakeholder management, this too must be planned. The work so far—from identifying stakeholders through to the development of a plan for their management—is an important starting point. However, this should be taken further, in the form of a *communication plan*, which is where we now turn our attention.

Communication Management

Poor communication is a major factor in project failure, and thus a robust plan can avoid some of the problems in ensuring all stakeholders—the customer(s), the project team, and all other stakeholders—have the information they need to contribute effectively to the project. The communication plan will be used to govern and track the flow of information during the life of the project, ensuring the right information is communicated to the right people, in the right format, at the right time.

As noted above, the stakeholder analysis described previously provides a valuable foundation for this work. We have already considered who our stakeholders are and the management actions we wish to take. We can now take this further to consider the form the communication will take and when and how frequently it will take place. It is logical that those stakeholders identified for close management will be communicated with more frequently, in more detail and, most likely, with more direct contact.

Stakeholders should be engaged as part of the planning process to assist with determining their information needs and when they need to be informed. Senior leaders will have different information needs from project team members and again from external stakeholders. We must determine who needs to be informed when changes are made to the project scope, or when the project reaches a particular milestone, or when there is an issue with a deliverable, for example.

Further to this, consideration must be given to how this information is disseminated. Face-to-face communication is the most effective in most circumstances, with the least scope for the message to be misconstrued. Some stakeholder relationships will be built on an expectation for this mode of communication. It is, however, clearly the most time intensive and effortful. Equally, copying everyone on an email will also not reap the best results. Information provision in an accurate and timely manner must be balanced with cost, time, and resources, since many of these communication outputs, such as reports, must also be included in the project scope. We can consider the following (Kloppenborg et al., 2019):

- Communicate accurately: not only being factually honest but also presenting information in a manner that people are likely to interpret correctly.
- Communicate promptly: providing the information soon enough so that it is useful to the recipient to facilitate timely decisions. For this reason, the communication plan includes a 'timing/frequency' field.
- Communicate effectively: the extent to which the receiver opens, understands, and acts appropriately upon the communication.

Finally, the plan should also detail who will be responsible for disseminating the information. As per our discussion of responsibility in the context of the RACI chart (refer to Chapter 5), caution should be taken to delegate this responsibility amongst the project team, as appropriate.

By building a plan around these details, we can proactively control the provision of information, rather than reacting to requests from stakeholders. We can establish a shared understanding of who will receive and send what information, when, and by what medium. A simple example communication plan is shown in Figure 6.3.

The importance of establishing a plan for project communication cannot be overstated. Many of the problems that plague a project can be attributed to a lack of clarity around a robust internal communication plan (Larson and Gray, 2018). "Communication leads to cooperation, which leads to coordination, which leads to project harmony, which leads to project success" (Badiru, 2008).

116 *Stakeholder and Communication Management*

Information	Stakeholder Group(s)	Method	Timing/ Frequency	Responsible
Project status updates	Project Team, Customer	Email	Weekly	Project Manager
Financial performance, strategic updates	Investors, Senior leadership Team	Email, Investor portal	Quarterly reports, AGM as scheduled	Project Manager
Order status, payment updates	Suppliers	Email, Phone	As needed •	Procurement Manager
Compliance reports, regulatory updates	Regulatory Bodies	Email, Letter	As required by regulations	Quality Manager
Community events, volunteering opportunities	Community members	Social media	Weekly	Community Manager

Figure 6.3 Example Communication Plan.

Summary

Stakeholders are a major part of project life. Projects have many diverse stakeholders, often wanting different things and carrying different expectations. This is why stakeholder management, and its planning, is such an important element of the project process.

We have examined who stakeholders are and how to identify them, analyse them, and plan for their involvement in a project. Importantly, we have looked beyond the process to also discuss the Project Manager as the person in the middle of stakeholder engagement and the practices and competencies they should develop to support this responsibility. Notions of both the Project Manager's role and project success have, in recent years, moved increasingly away from a singular focus on the Project Management Triangle towards consideration of engagement with, and satisfaction of, stakeholders, respectively. The ability to build relationships and communicate effectively are at the heart of reconciling the diversity of stakeholders and the hugely significant role they can play in a project's fortunes.

Finally, we have also examined the communication management process, building on the work around stakeholder management, arriving at a communication plan and an understanding of why this is so important to project success.

References

Ackermann, F. and Eden, C. (2011). Strategic Management of Stakeholders: Theory and Practice, *Long Range Planning*, 44(3), pp. 179–196.

Ancona, D., Malone, T.W., Orlikowski, W.J. and Senge, P.M. (2007). In Praise of the Incomplete Leader, *Harvard Business Review*, 85(2), p. 92.

Badiru, A.B. (2008). *Triple C Model of Project Management: Communication, Cooperation, and Coordination*, Boca Raton, FL: CRC Press.

Bourne, L. (2015). *Making Projects Work: Effective Stakeholder and Communication Management*, Boca Raton, FL: CRC Press.

Eden, C. and Ackermann, F. (1998). *Making Strategy: The Journey of Strategic Management*, London: Sage Publications.

Eskerod, P. and Jepsen, A.L. (2013). *Project Stakeholder Management*, Aldershot: Gower.

Eskerod, P., Huemann, M. and Ringhofer, C. (2015). Stakeholder Inclusiveness: Enriching Project Management with General Stakeholder Theory, *Project Management Journal*, 46(6), pp. 42–53.

Goleman, D. (2004). *Primal Leadership: How to Lead with Emotional Intelligence*, Cambridge, MA: Harvard Business School Press.

Kloppenborg, T., Anantatmula, V. and Wells, K. (2019). *Contemporary Project Management* (4th ed.), Boston, MA: Cengage.

Larson, E.W. and Gray, C.F. (2018). *Project Management: The Managerial Process* (7th ed.), New York, NY: McGraw-Hill Education.

Merrow, E.W. and Nandurdikar, N. (2018). *Leading Complex Projects: A Data-Driven Approach to Mastering the Human Side of Project Management*, Oxford: Wiley.

Miller, D. and Oliver, M. (2015). *Engaging Stakeholders for Project Success*, PMI White Paper, Newtown Square, PA: Project Management Institute.

Mitchell, R., Agle, B. and Wood, D. (1997). Toward a Theory of Stakeholder Identification and Salience: Defining the Principle of Who and What Really Counts, *The Academy of Management Review*, 22(4), pp. 853–886.

Wells, K. and Kloppenborg, T. (2015). *Project Management Essentials*, New York, NY: Business Expert Press.

7 Project Executing

Introduction

In this chapter, the *Executing* stage of a project is explored. Having developed a plan, that plan must now be executed. We know, however, that change is an inevitable part of project life, and thus much of the focus in this chapter is on how to identify the need for change and enact it. We discuss why project variances against the plan occur and how these can be detected (termed 'project monitoring') and responses to it managed (termed 'project control'). We examine *earned value analysis* as a technique for measuring performance of the project over time. We also address how performance should be reported to the project's stakeholders. Finally, we discuss the importance of effective communication in identifying issues early and resolving them effectively.

The Plan-Monitor-Control Cycle

With Waterfall projects, it is often said that we first 'plan the work' and then 'work the plan'. It is the latter that we now focus on. However, project execution is never this simple, and the Project Manager must adapt in response to changes. It has taken a great amount of time, effort, and resources to reach this point—an executable project plan—so we must ensure we now proactively monitor and control against it.

As the project transitions from the period of planning the work to actually doing the work, the *plan-monitor-control cycle*

DOI: 10.4324/9781003057246-7

must be engaged (Figure 7.1). Up to this point, we have spent a lot of time planning and establishing baselines in the form of a schedule, budget, work breakdown structure, etc. As that work is executed, we must track the progress of the work activities in an accurate and timely manner (often with the support of software solutions). Importantly, the actual performance must be measured against what was planned; this process is termed *project monitoring*. Any difference between the two is known as a *variance*. When a variance is identified, we must take action to either bring the project back in line with the plan or, if that is not possible, revise the plan. The processes, decisions, and actions involved in responding to variances are known collectively as *project control*. Where replanning is required, this would engage the change management process (previously described in Chapter 4). We examine both project monitoring and project control further in later sections of this chapter.

The plan-monitor-control cycle is continuously employed for the remainder of the project's life. It should look familiar. We have discussed the importance of monitoring, controlling, and (re)planning in earlier chapters of this book. In the context

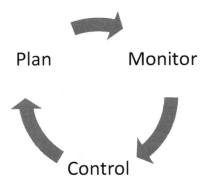

Plan   Monitor

Control

Figure 7.1 The Plan-Monitor-Control Cycle.

of risk, we discussed the importance of tracking and controlling risk management actions and updating the risk register as necessary. Similarly, when discussing stakeholder management, we highlighted the need to regularly review and reassess—or monitor, control, and potentially revise—the stakeholder plan due to the dynamic nature of stakeholder relations. This is similar and calls for project managers to be equally proactive in the duties of monitoring and control.

Why Do Variances Happen?

There are a number of different factors we can point to—some avoidable, some not—that collectively lead to variances occurring on a project. Variances are a natural part of project life in execution, but what is particularly harmful to projects are the patterns of variances that will lead to more and more being generated over time if the root cause is not addressed. The potential causes below can serve as a checklist for project managers seeking to better understand why variances may be occurring on their project:

- *Poor Estimating:* of the duration, resource requirements, budgetary requirements, risk exposure, and/or dependencies of project activities.
- *Scope Creep:* as discussed in Chapter 4, this refers to unauthorised or uncontrolled change, leading the scope to expand over time. Closely related to this is *feature creep*, which sees team members adding features and functions to the deliverable that they think the customer wants even though it is not included in the requirements or WBS (Wysocki, 2019). If changes are being made without engaging the change management process, this is likely a case of scope or feature creep.
- *Parkinson's Law:* the observation that work expands to fill the time available for its completion (Parkinson, 1955). This inevitably leads to work sometimes running over schedule despite adequate time being assigned to it.

- *Student Syndrome:* perhaps unfairly named, since we are all prone to procrastinate at times, this describes how someone might only start to apply themselves to a task at the last possible moment before a deadline (Goldratt, 2017). Some people need the pressure of an impending deadline to motivate them. It does however often lead to missed deadlines or incomplete or poor-quality work.
- *Escalation of Commitment:* the human behaviour that sees an individual or a group persist with a particular course of action in the face of negative outcomes (Staw, 1997). On projects, project personnel can increasingly become anchored to past decisions and be reluctant to change opinion or approach. Away from project variances, the same phenomenon sees organisations continuing to invest time, money, and resources into projects when there is minimal chance of them succeeding (the 'sunk cost' fallacy of "throwing good money after bad"; Parayre, 1995)

Of course, there are also those changes that could not have been avoided. We can refer to Murphy's Law here: "anything that can go wrong, will go wrong". This is a guiding principle behind effective risk management as we proactively identify and assess all those things that could go wrong on the project. Even with the most robust approach to risk management, not everything will go to plan. What is important then is how we identify and deal with the things that go wrong: monitoring and controlling. This is where we now turn our attention.

Project Monitoring

Project monitoring refers to any process or system for identifying variances from the original plan. Data is collected, analysed, and reported so as to provide the Project Manager, project team, and the project's stakeholders with answers to questions such as (Larson and Gray, 2018):

- What is the project's current status in terms of schedule and cost?
- How much will it cost to complete the project?
- When will the project be completed?
- Are there potential problems that need to be addressed now?
- What, who, and where are the causes of cost or schedule overruns?

Whilst we address project monitoring here, in project execution, this is of course another element of the project that must be carefully planned. The Project Manager must consider the following in the design of the monitoring system (Maylor and Turner, 2022):

- *What will be measured:* to determine what is of greatest importance to this particular project. Most projects do not have the resources to closely track everything, and thus there is a need to prioritise. Ultimately, this should already be known from the project's requirements and typically falls on time, cost, resource usage, and quality (although other factors such as health and safety, legal, ethical, environmental, etc. should also be considered). Which of these is most critical will determine which should be most closely monitored. This will also be where the greatest focus for control activities is placed. Whilst it can be tempting to measure what is easily gathered, the focus must be on that which is important for controlling the project. It is also important to measure both the input (i.e. budget spent, time elapsed) and the output (i.e. percent of work complete), since the former is not a reliable proxy for the latter (Meredith et al., 2017).
- *The limits of variation:* to establish the tolerance for deviation from the plan. For some factors (e.g. health and safety, environmental), a zero tolerance might be appropriate. For others, such as budget, a one percent overspend might not

be a problem. This includes highlighting both negative and positive variances. Any negative variation should trigger further monitoring to ensure the situation does not worsen.

- *When to measure:* to arrive at a balance between diligence in monitoring and giving project personnel the space to complete their work. When there is a problem, we need to identify it quickly, but this should not lead us to permanently bother people for an update on their progress. The timing of the observation and the speed of reaction are both important here. Progress can be monitored continuously (supported by software) or upon reaching milestones/stage gates/review points.

Further to this is how progress and performance are reported, which we will address in a later section of this chapter.

Project monitoring on low complexity projects might require only a simple checklist; on highly complex projects, a more robust and detailed system will be required. We will examine a variety of performance measures here for project monitoring; it is then for the Project Manager to determine which of these is most appropriate for their project.

Checklists and Variance Data Tracking

The most straightforward approaches require maintaining a simple spreadsheet to track progress to date. A checklist can be used to monitor those activities that are closed, in progress, and not started, along with start and end dates. This can be taken further by tracking the variance of the start/end dates with those that were in the project plan. A similar approach can be utilised to monitor cost and resource expenditure.

Tracking Charts

Earlier in the project, we established the timing, cost, and resource requirements of each activity on the WBS. In execution, a tracking chart can be produced that presents a comparison of this data and actual progress. An example is shown in Figure 7.2 for tracking schedule progress.

An advantage of showing this data graphically, as opposed to in a spreadsheet, is that it supports the identification of a variance trend over time. We can see if things are getting worse, and rather than simply asking 'how can we get back on track', we can instead look to identify the root cause(s) of the recurring issue, thus leading to more effective corrective action.

Similar charts, termed 'burn charts', can be produced to analyse the cumulative consumption of resources (e.g. budget or labour hours) over time. An example is shown in Figure 7.3: the project here is consistently, albeit modestly, over-consuming budget.

For a more advanced representation of actual and planned resource consumption, earned value analysis (EVA) can be used, which tracks both schedule and cost in a single metric of project performance.

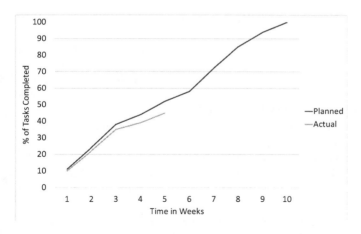

Figure 7.2 Example Tracking Chart (Time and Task Completion).

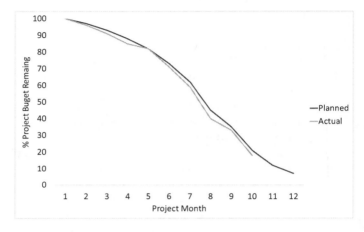

Figure 7.3 Burn Chart (Time and Task Completion).

Earned Value Analysis

The preceding measures of performance have a significant shortcoming in that they only contrast two of three measures at one time out of work complete, cost, and schedule. Projects can be succeeding on one or two of these dimensions but really struggling on another. For example, it is very possible for a project to be 70% complete but to have spent 95% of its budget. EVA addresses this shortcoming by capturing work complete, cost, and schedule together.

EVA relies on a detailed schedule and costings for the entire project. A WBS should have been developed, the activities of which were sequenced, scheduled, and assigned a budget (as described in Chapters 4 and 5). This allows us to create a time-phased budget for the project: at any point in time, we know how much work should be complete and how much it should have cost to complete that work. This is termed the *planned value* (PV): the amount planned to be spent by any given project date. In execution, we collect the costs accumulated by completing the work, which is our *actual cost* (AC). The *earned value* (EV) is the budgeted cost of the work performed up to a specified date. It disregards actual costs incurred and reflects only what the work complete was budgeted to cost. EV is calculated by multiplying the budgeted cost of the work at the end of the project (BAC) by the percentage of task completion (EV = BAC × % complete). We can then calculate the schedule variance (SV = EV − PV) and cost variance (CV = EV − AC). A positive variance indicates the project is in a desirable position, whereas a negative variance suggests there are problems to be addressed.

It is important to note that SV does not reflect the critical path, and the only accurate method to determine the true time progress of the project is to compare the planned and actual network schedules (Larson and Gray, 2018). SV is, however, a useful indicator of the overall direction the project is taking.

The various terms are summarised in Figure 7.4.

Question	Answer	Initialism
How much work should be done?	Planned value	PV
How much work is done?	Earned value	EV
How much did the completed work cost?	Actual cost	AC
What was the total budget for the project?	Budget at completion	BAC
How much is the project schedule ahead/behind?	Schedule variance	SV
How much is the project over/under budget?	Cost variance	CV

Figure 7.4 EVA Terminology (Adapted from Kloppenborg et al., 2019).

Example 7.1   Earned Value Analysis

A project with a total budget (BAC) of £20,000 is six months into its ten-month schedule. Actual expenditure to date (AC) is £13,500 having completed 55% of the project scope. The planned expenditure by month was as follows:

Month	Monthly Expenditure (£)	Cumulative Expenditure (£)
1	500	500
2	750	1,250
3	1,250	2,500
4	2,500	5,000
5	3,000	8,000
6	4,000	12,000
7	5,000	17,000
8	1,500	18,500
9	1,000	19,500
10	500	20,000

You have been asked to determine the status of the project.

- $PV = £12,000$
- $EV = \%$ completion $\times BAC = 0.55 \times £20,000 = £11,000$
- $SV = EV - PV = £11,000 - £12,000 = -£1,000$

SV can also be expressed as a percentage:
- $SV\% = SV/EV = 9\%$ behind schedule

- $CV = EV - AC = 11,000 - 13,500 = -£2,500$
- $CV\% = CV/EV = 23\%$ over planned cost

The data can also be presented graphically as shown in Figure 7.5.

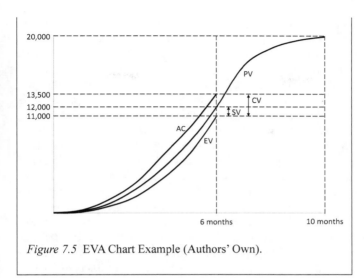

Figure 7.5 EVA Chart Example (Authors' Own).

Further to this, we can also capture two performance indexes—schedule performance index (SPI = EV/PV) and cost performance index (CPI = EV/AC)—which measure how close the project is to performing to schedule and budget, respectively. This allows us to forecast the predicted cost and schedule impact of any variance to completion: the BAC or planned duration of the project (for cost and schedule, respectively) is simply divided by the performance index. For example, a project with a planned duration of four months with an SPI of 0.8 will be delivered in five months unless corrective action is taken. A project with a BAC of £5,000 and a CPI of 0.5 will cost £10,000 without corrective action.

CPI and SPI are preferred for reporting purposes in particular since it is simple to equate each index to a baseline of 1 (a value less than 1 is undesirable, whereas a value greater than 1 shows strong performance). For this reason, they are also often used by organisations as benchmarks for comparing the performance of a number of projects within a portfolio.

A notable challenge with EVA is in estimating the percentage completion of a task (and collectively, a project). As a result, there are several competing conventions to estimating progress. The most popular is 50–50, whereby the task is listed as 50% complete once initiated and 100% once completed. Clearly, this approach overstates the EV of those tasks that have just been initiated but understates that of those nearing completion. A variation on this is to not ascribe any value greater than zero until a task is complete; the challenge being that a project will always appear to be 'behind schedule' (Wysocki, 2019). Another is to base percentage completion on either the proportion of that task's budget that has currently been spent or the task's duration that has currently elapsed (or a combination of the two). However, neither of these measures are accurate indicators of progress. Perhaps the most 'objective' approach is to establish frequent monitoring points over the duration of work packages and use units completed (e.g. lines of code, labour hours, bricks laid, etc.) to assign costs and measure progress (Larson and Gray, 2018).

A project that appears on paper to be just a little over budget and a little behind schedule can, once EVA is applied, look in much greater trouble once the true picture is clear. The utility of EVA is not solely in reporting current progress but also in predicting how problematic performance to date can lead to cost and schedule overruns at the project's completion (or even whether it will have the budget and/or schedule slack to complete at all). It is a very powerful tool and, if applied consistently throughout execution, can assist in the detection of issues and their rectification.

Project Reporting

A significant part of collecting and analysing data on project performance and progress is to also report it to various stakeholder groups. The provision of accurate, clear, and timely information allows those groups to make decisions concerning the project and maintains their support in it. This may include, for example, status reports (an overview of the entire project's progress against the plan at that point in time), progress reports (which focus on the progress of specific activities and milestones), and forecasts (perhaps as the result of EVA). These can be issued either at regular intervals or upon reaching a particular milestone. Kloppenborg et al. (2019) suggest reporting must be made across three time horizons:

- *The past:* the immediate period between the last report or meeting and now. Reporting on what was planned and what was accomplished. Any variance between the two should be addressed.
- *The present:* the period from now until the next report or meeting. What will be accomplished in this time period, what risks and issues are foreseen, and what changes need to be approved?
- *The future:* the time horizon after the next reporting period. What future risks and issues are envisioned and how will these be addressed? Are further changes anticipated?

The frequency and the content of the report must be tailored to the specific audience: the project team will need more detailed information, more regularly (and likely delivered informally) than external stakeholders (e.g. senior leaders, sponsors, clients). Meetings, informal conversations, and project reviews are also all a mainstay of the reporting process.

Beyond project control, there are numerous other benefits to delivering detailed, timely reports to the right people (Meredith et al., 2017):

- Establishing a shared understanding with stakeholders regarding the goals, progress, difficulties, successes, and other ongoing events of importance;
- Communicating the need for coordination among different teams and sub-teams working on the tasks of the project;
- Maintaining a communication network for global projects;
- Communicating changes, when made, in a timely manner, thus minimising confusion;
- Maintaining the visibility of the project, and the project team, to senior leaders, functional managers, colleagues, and clients;
- Keeping the project team motivated (unless the project is a disaster).

Whilst reports have been a mainstay of project life for decades, the more recent utilisation of real-time data in project management has introduced the possibility to report control information as it happens. With more frequent reporting comes the opportunity to respond more quickly to any issues. 'Digital dashboards' can be created, using a traffic light system to show how particular activities are progressing (e.g. green if within 2% of schedule and budget; amber if within 5% of schedule and budget; red if beyond 5% of schedule and budget). These are particularly effective where teams are in multiple sites or locations (Maylor and Turner, 2022). If applied across an organisation's portfolio, data from individual projects can be rolled up to offer senior leaders insights into the contrasting performance of different projects. Of course, these systems rely on the quality and veracity of the information collected: we have heard stories of 'watermelon projects', which are reported as green but are really red on the inside.

Project Control

The final stage of the plan-monitor-control cycle concerns any act for reducing variances between planned and actual progress. In truth, much of the planning activities discussed in earlier chapters are about control: we develop a WBS, critical path analysis, a detailed schedule, plans for stakeholder and risk management, etc. all with the aim of 'controlling' the future of the project. We know, however, that things will not go according to plan, no matter how well the project has been planned, and thus we must respond to problems when they arise. This requires taking both effective and timely action in the face of issues before they become serious problems. Further, it calls for the Project Manager to take a systemic perspective on these issues, seeking out trends and patterns that might lead to a root cause to also be addressed.

There is both a process and a people side to project control. With regards to the former, there may be a need to capture further risks, change the project schedule, or make a request for expedited delivery from a supplier, for example. On the people side, execution is an acutely pressurised period of project life, where people are operating under exact deadlines and emotions can run high. An effective Project Manager will be able to lead on both fronts. We will discuss people management further towards the end of this chapter in a discussion of the problem of silence in execution. On the process side, there are several possible responses to project variances detected through project monitoring:

- Shorten (or 'crash') remaining critical activities to bring the project on track with initial plans and commitments, usually by assigning further human resources or increasing the labour hours in a working day/week (refer to Chapter 5).
- Negotiate a new due date with the customer to manage expectations about project delays.

- Provide appropriate assistance to teams whose activities have undesirable variances.
- Work with suppliers (internal and external) to ensure on-time or expedited delivery of critical materials.
- Re-evaluate the WBS to consider reducing the project scope (also discussed in Chapter 5).
- Revise the project schedule, budget, or both, if scope or specifications have legitimately changed.
- Evaluate whether variances are the result of scope creep and, if so, ensure the change management process is followed from hereon.

As the above suggests, a significant part of effective project control is having a systematic process for requesting, reviewing, documenting, and tracking changes. Managing change is undoubtedly one of the most challenging aspects of the job for any Project Manager: a study of over 500 project managers examining the things that bothered them most in their role found the top response to be coping with changes (Meredith et al., 2017). A robust system can help with the inevitable change that comes with executing a project.

It is similarly vital to detect issues early, as generally these only get worse whilst they go undetected, and the cost and difficulty of making changes increases as the project progresses. There will be 'early warning signs' that a variance may be about to occur, which, if detected, allows us to act early whilst the effects are small and the issue can be more easily managed. Early warning signs can save a project from disaster (if appropriate action is taken) but too often they are detected very late, often leaving no room for action (Alaskar, 2013). As with the Project Manager's role in project control, early warning signs require a focus on both project processes and people. With regards to process, perhaps there is information missing from reports, risks that have been poorly identified, or a lack of documented requirements. In people, we might observe poor communication amongst our team and/or stakeholders, an uneasy atmosphere in the office, or high or low presenteeism (both of which can be indicators that something is wrong). We expect our project managers to be faithful to the project plans and underlying processes; this should be combined with the emotional intelligence (discussed in Chapter 6) to understand people, build relationships, and identify changes in behaviour that might lead to problems. We will examine this further now.

Silence in Execution

The pace of progress in Executing, combined with the project being considerably larger than it was in Planning (e.g. more personnel, more stakeholders, more businesses, more locations), make it easier for issues to remain hidden until it is too late. The answer, then, lies in breaking 'a code of silence' around difficult conversations. The most notable proponents of this concept are Grenny et al. (2007, 2013), following 150 hours of observational research and interviews, surveys, and focus groups of over 1,000 senior leaders, project sponsors, project managers, and project personnel across over 2,200 projects. Their research highlights five highly common yet largely ignored problems, which they posit as questions (which they term "crucial conversations"). What determines whether these five problems will derail a project is whether they can be discussed openly:

1 *Are we planning around facts?* Plans may have been made based on unrealistic commitments around deadlines, cost, and project scope. A set of unrealistic project parameters is highly likely to bring the final project in over budget, past schedule, and of poor quality, unless confronted by the Project Manager and their team, often in conversation with the sponsors and customer.
2 *Is the Project Sponsor providing support?* We discussed in Chapter 2 the important role of the Project Sponsor. Project teams will require the support of the sponsor, particularly

in this highly challenging stage of project life. Over 75% of projects with weak sponsorship finish significantly over budget, behind schedule, and below specifications. If that support has been withdrawn, it must be discussed with the objective of confirming the sponsor once again in an active role on the project.

3 *Are we faithful to the process?* Stakeholders and senior leaders often ignore the formal project processes so as to not be burdened by them. However, those processes exist for a reason: consider the importance of a formalised process for managing change, risk, stakeholders, scheduling, and budgeting, etc. This can leave projects under-resourced, victim to scope creep, and with low morale.

4 *Are we honestly assessing our progress and risks?* New risks will continue to emerge and must be discussed openly. Individuals will sometimes refrain from discussing risks and issues for fear of being blamed or seen as negative. The same is true with progress. By not reporting honestly, we lose the opportunity to take corrective action.

5 *Are team members pulling their weight?* Project leaders often do not have adequate say in who they hire or whether those who are underperforming can be replaced. Correcting this requires strong communication with the project's sponsors and the organisation's senior leaders.

When problems, such as these, are discussed openly, they can be addressed through corrective action. Problems that go undetected will build and build until they land with a thud, derailing the project and possibly leading to its failure. Project managers should thus strive to develop a culture of openness and honesty, grounded in trust and effective communication.

Summary

In this chapter, we have examined each element of the plan-monitor-control cycle in turn. It is important that this cycle continues to operate throughout the execution stage. Not everything will go to plan, and thus replanning is a crucial component of effectively executing a project. We have discussed various methods for project monitoring, with a particular focus on earned value analysis, along with some best practice around its reporting. We have also addressed how project variances are responded to through project control.

Much of the discussion in this chapter has focused on the process side of executing a project, but importantly, we have also addressed the people side, particularly in our discussion of early warning signs and focused conversations. We can draw your attention to one notorious quote from renowned computer scientist Fred Brooks (1975):

"How does a project get one year late? … One day at a time"

This speaks to the importance of early detection of variances and then acting on them, and this requires us to rely on both robust processes and the people around us.

References

Alaskar, A.H. (2013). Managing Troubled Projects. Paper presented at *PMI Global Congress 2013 North America*, New Orleans, LA. Newtown Square, PA: Project Management Institute.

Brooks, F.P. (1975). *The Mythical Man-Month: Essays on Software Engineering*, Reading, MA: Addison-Wesley.

Goldratt, E.M. (2017). *Critical Chain: A Business Novel*, Oxford: Gower.

Grenny, J., Maxfield, D.G. and Shimberg, A. (2007). How Project Leaders Can Overcome the Crisis of Silence, *Sloan Management Review*, 48, pp. 46–52.

Grenny, J., Maxfield, D.G., Shimberg, A. and McMillan, R. (2013). Silence Fails: Five Crucial Conversations for Flawless Execution. Paper presented at *PMI Global Congress 2013 North America,* New Orleans, LA. Newtown Square, PA: Project Management Institute.

Kloppenborg, T., Anantatmula, V. and Wells, K. (2019). *Contemporary Project Management* (4th ed.), Boston, MA: Cengage.

Larson, E.W. and Gray, C.F. (2018). *Project Management: The Managerial Process* (7th ed.), New York, NY: McGraw-Hill Education.

Maylor, H. and Turner, N. (2022). *Project Management* (5th ed.), Harlow: Pearson.

Meredith, J.R., Shafer, S.M. and Mantel Jr., S.J. (2017). *Project Management in Practice* (6th ed.), Hoboken, NJ: Wiley.

Parayre, R. (1995). The Strategic Implications of Sunk Costs: A Behavioural Perspective, *Journal of Economic Behaviour and Organisation*, 28(3), pp. 417–442.

Parkinson, C.N. (1955). Parkinson's Law, *The Economist*, 19 (November), pp. 635–637.

Staw, B.M. (1997). The Escalation of Commitment: An Update and Appraisal. In: Shapira Z. (ed.), *Organizational Decision Making*, pp. 191–215, New York, NY: Cambridge University Press.

Wysocki, R.K. (2019). *Effective Project Management: Traditional, Agile, Extreme, Hybrid* (8th ed.), Indianapolis, IN: Wiley.

8 Project Closing

Introduction

This final chapter addresses the closing stage of the project lifecycle. Too often, project closure is rushed so as to move on to the next project. However, to do so is at the detriment to the organisation, given the potential here to strengthen stakeholder relationships and reflect on the project experience, including capturing lessons learned, so that future projects can benefit from this insight. We discuss why projects might close prematurely, before focusing on the formal process for project closure. We address the requirement to effectively transition deliverables to the customer and the finalisation and handover of project documentation. We also discuss the significance of the post-project review.

Project Closing

Projects are by definition temporary endeavours, and all come to an end. This either occurs upon completion of the project's objectives, or otherwise for any number of other reasons that lead to its premature closure. Regardless of the nature of project closure, there is undoubtedly a right way to do it. There are three guiding principles: first, to ensure any deliverables are handed over to the responsible party and formally documenting the project's closure; secondly, to evaluate the project's performance against the objectives established during the project's initiation; and finally, to maximise the opportunity for organisational

DOI: 10.4324/9781003057246-8

learning stemming from the project experience by conducting project reviews and capturing lessons learned. The latter is an area in which organisations often fall down to the detriment of future project performance. We will address each of these in turn over the course of this chapter, but first turn our attention to the subject of premature project closure.

Premature Project Close

Projects do not always end as was planned. Rather than being viewed as a negative thing, this should more suitably be considered as a good organisational decision that prevents further investment being made into a project that is unlikely to yield the desired benefits (APM, 2019). Indeed, this can be viewed as a positive organisational capability. There are several reasons that a project might be closed before its intended finish date, such as (Lock, 2013):

- The project is deemed to no longer have a viable business case.
- The parent organisation has run out of funds, killing the project.
- The parent organisation wishes to make fundamental changes, causing the project to be scrapped or restarted.
- Economic or political conditions have changed, meaning the project is no longer financially viable for the parent organisation in the foreseeable future.
- The customer asks for the project to be 'put on hold' (i.e. delayed indefinitely), pending a possible improvement in market conditions or to await the results of a reappraisal.
- Government policy changes result in the termination of some government contracts (defence contracts for weapons systems, aircraft, etc. are always subject to such risks).
- An Act of God (e.g. flood) has intervened, causing further work on the project to be suspended or abandoned.
- Hostile activities have broken out in an internal or international conflict, making work on the project impossible.

Premature closure may affect the type of project closing process required. However, the practice of transitioning deliverables (as appropriate), evaluating the project and capturing lessons learned—as outlined in this chapter—is nevertheless important when closing a project prematurely.

Formal Project Close

Project management does not end abruptly once execution has been completed, and there are several important processes that must be carried out within project closure to ensure the effective handover of deliverables, evaluation of perform-ance, and capturing of lessons learned. The temptation might be to move on to the next project as soon as possible, but doing so does not ensure that the maximum benefit is yielded from the current project's experience. As such, a significant part of these closure activities is focused on learning. For the Project Manager, closure activities include (Maylor, 2010):

• Ensuring there is an incentive for the project to be finished and that activities are completed.
• Ensuring documentation of the process is provided to allow review, as is documentation of the outcome to facilitate any future support activities.
• Closing down the project systems (e.g. accounting systems) on projects where dedicated systems have been used.
• Constructing the immediate review of activities, providing a starting point for all improvement activities.
• Appraisal and relocation of staff who have completed their activities and disposal of assets that are surplus to requirements.
• Ensuring that all stakeholders are satisfied: sell your achievements and maximise the business benefit from the project.

We will address this process by grouping these and other closure activities into three themes that we will explore in turn: (i) transitioning deliverables and documentation; (ii) evaluating project performance and capturing lessons learned; and (iii) post-project review.

Transitioning Deliverables and Documentation

A significant part of project closure is ensuring the project's customer(s) are satisfied and able to use the project outputs. After all, a well-satisfied customer may be essential to securing future projects and ensuring an otherwise successful project is deemed a success. In the first instance, the project needs to attain 'delivery acceptance' of the project outputs from the customer. Customer involvement, as we have already discussed, is paramount to project success, and if that principle has been applied through the lifecycle, then the project outputs should be useful for the customer, and this process should be free of surprises.

The conditions for attaining acceptance and handing over deliverables should be clearly defined, agreed with the customer, and documented at the beginning of the project. The APM (2019) encourages organisations to conduct a 'change impact analysis' to understand the activities required to support the project's outputs. This will identify the potential impacts of the project on the organisation as well as gaps in knowledge and skill that need to be addressed. As this suggests, the provision of additional support may be required to aid the customer in bringing the project outputs into beneficial use (such as instructions, user guides, demonstrations, training, and technical support).

Customer acceptance should be formally recorded, often as the result of a *scope verification* process. This can be performed internally at first, verifying all the work has been completed on the project in reference to the project charter, scope statement, WBS, and/or schedule. Many organisations utilise checklists that itemise all project activities and/or deliverables, including the assignment of responsibilities. Thereafter, scope verification can be conducted with the customer/end user. Kloppenborg

(2009) offers the example of a construction company with the buyers of a new home: before closing out the project, you would demonstrate to the buyers the various features they were offered and how things work. The buyers would try the light switches, look at the finish, and consider all the things they agreed to pay for in the house. Any outstanding issues are recorded as a 'punch list' of items to be completed by an agreed later date. The customer will then formally accept the project output(s), subject to any punch list items being completed.

In addition to the handover of project outputs is the finalisation and handover of project documentation. This can sometimes be hurried through an eagerness to move on to the next project. The activity might otherwise be a poor fit for project personnel that are typically very goal-oriented in their work. However, high-quality documentation will provide evidence that the project has been completed in a proper manner (to assist in the avoidance of litigation, and providing a starting point for review) and will support future project work in having a good starting point (as will be discussed further in the subsequent section; Maylor, 2010). This really should be a case of *finalising* documentation, as documentation should have been produced and maintained throughout the life of the project. If left until too late, much will go unrecorded and leave the organisation exposed to litigation and inefficiencies in the future.

The closure itself can be finalised through a 'project closure document': a simple form that typically contains information such as the project title, project number, closure date, reason for closure, any special instructions, distribution, and an authorising signature (Lock, 2013). The ownership of the documentation is then transferred to the customer or parent organisation accordingly.

Evaluating Project Performance and Lessons Learned

A further important element of effective project closure is reflecting on how things went on the project, commending project personnel on their contribution, and considering how this might inform future project practice. In the first instance, an immediate project review should be conducted at the time of project closure. This is distinct from post-project reviews, which aim to assess a project's impact once its outputs have been operationalised and outcomes can be measured (discussed in the subsequent section). The immediate project review should collate initial reflections on the project and any immediate remedial/improvement action that may be required, so as to provide rapid feedback on the performance of the project team, systems, and processes that were used. This should be made against specific criteria and standards, established before commencement of the project. Organisations should consider evaluating the team-building process, effectiveness of group discussion and problem-solving processes, team cohesiveness and trust, and customer satisfaction with project deliverables (Larson and Gray, 2018).

This is often extended to also include individual appraisals of project personnel, prior to project members being allocated to their next assignments. This should: inform the individual of the aspects of their performance that should be repeated; allow the organisation to assess the utility of individuals to future teams; and aid managers in identifying training or educational requirements for the organisation (Maylor, 2010). In general, individual performance reviews centre around the technical and social skills that have contributed to the project and its team (Larson and Gray, 2018). Such reviews can also be a useful platform for project leadership to offer support and guidance to those seeking new opportunities. Many project managers highlight the importance of such activities to strengthening personal ties and building a network of competent people who can be called upon to participate in future projects (Maylor, 2010).

The core purpose of a project is to create something unique, often with a unique group of people brought together as a team, all working towards a common goal. That makes for an excellent environment to create new knowledge. Perhaps a new product, technology, methodology, process, or revenue stream has emerged from this project, which can then be shared with the wider organisation and used again in future project work. Equally, the things that did not go well on the project also have value to the organisation. This knowledge should be captured in the form of 'lessons learned'. Importantly, it belongs to the project team, not the individuals, and a common mistake of many projects is not capturing the lessons learned before moving the team members on to their next assignments. Once the team is disbanded, much of the knowledge is lost.

Whilst we discuss lessons learned here in the context of project closure, recording and sharing lessons learned should actually be a mainstay of project work throughout the lifecycle. Nevertheless, project closure presents an important and final opportunity to capture additional lessons learned in reflection of the project experience as a whole. The Project Manager may choose to run 'post-mortem' meetings with project personnel to discuss what went well, what went badly, and any recommendations stemming from this, as well as reflections on the project management method, project approaches and controls, and any abnormal events that caused deviation from the plan (Murray, 2017).

Further to capturing the lessons learned is the dissemination of them to the wider organisation. In our experience, organisations are generally quite effective at collecting lessons learned but fall down in actually utilising them. Best practice involves a shared, searchable database, with assigned responsibilities within the organisation for its maintenance. Each lesson should also have an owner (including the owner's contact details) so that future project personnel can discuss the lesson with them. Moreover, lessons learned need to be part of the organisational culture, with clear incentives and support for capturing lessons learned, and the promotion of adopting organisational lessons learned on current projects. After all, lessons learned only have value if they are used and become *lessons applied.*

Post-Project Review

The ultimate aim of a project is not to generate project outputs but rather outcomes and benefits from those outputs. As such, it is certainly a worthwhile endeavour to conduct a review sometime after the closure of the project to measure to what extent the outcomes and strategic benefits that were anticipated from the project have actually been realised. As with the lessons learned process, the intent is to enhance the performance of future projects and support continuous improvement within the organisation.

Larson and Gray (2018) emphasise the importance of planning the review, so as to maximise its effectiveness and ensure efficient use of participants' time. An appropriate reviewer should also be allocated to oversee the review process: a suitable candidate would be the Project Sponsor. The role of the reviewer is important, requiring purposeful and objective leadership in making sense of conflicting information and being careful not to impart their own biases on the process. A collaborative, rather than adversarial, approach should be adopted, and this should also be informed by the past experience of both the reviewer and the organisation. A holistic perspective over the project should be adopted, considering evidence collectively and verifying it wherever possible (from both internal and external data sources).

The review should also consider the impact the project has had on the external environment (e.g. customer satisfaction, market share, brand awareness). Figure 8.1 illustrates a variety of criteria and corresponding methods of assessment. As per our discussion in Chapter 3 around project appraisal, there are many considerations here beyond financial factors, and these include both qualitative and quantitative measures.

The choice of which of these measures to adopt for the review should ultimately be determined by the project's objectives—as initially outlined in the business case—and the strategic objectives of the parent organisation. More generally, the business

Criteria	Review
Financial	ROI, cost variance
Time	Schedule variance
Quality	Customer perceptions and satisfaction
Human resources	Personnel, roles and responsibilities
Environmental	Environmental impact assessment
Planning	Cost, schedule, scope (inc. techniques used)
Control	Monitoring and control processes/systems

Figure 8.1 Post-Project Review Criteria (Adapted from Maylor, 2010).

case can be an invaluable input into this post-project review process.

What is not significantly addressed in the above set of measures is *personal experience,* and there can be great value in capturing this from the project's personnel. Some project management approaches, such as PRINCE2, encourage project managers to use a 'logbook' for recording personal reflections on project experience (thus highlighting the value of such reflections). Questions could be asked of key project personnel (and, potentially, stakeholders also) about the effectiveness of planning and control systems, the productiveness of stakeholder interfaces, how well the project was managed, how supportive the team culture was, and the level of organisational support and resourcing (i.e. people, budget, equipment, etc.).

A report should be generated from the output of the review, so as to collect the key insights from the process. This should include (Larson and Gray, 2018):

- *Classification* of the project by its key characteristics (e.g. type, size, number of staff, technology level).
- *Analysis* in the form of a set of summary statements about the project: its mission and objectives, procedures and systems used, organisational resources used, and outcomes achieved.
- *Recommendations* to the organisation, in a manner that speaks to the points addressed in the Analysis section (e.g. changes to how resources are allocated in the future, or a new procedure or system to pilot on a future project).
- *Lessons Learned,* given that this post-project review is an excellent further opportunity to capture these. These should, of course, also be captured and disseminated within the organisation further to this report in the manner described earlier in this chapter.

The post-project report should be retained by the PMO and made available as a valuable reference document for project-related questions that might later arise.

Summary

In our experience, organisations are far too hasty in closing down a project and reallocating its personnel to other endeavours. This ultimately results in a great deal of knowledge, accumulated over months or years, being lost that might have had significant value to the organisation and its pursuit of continuous improvement. Of the three crucial processes we have outlined in this chapter, two are focused on *learning* by objectively assessing performance, *reflecting* on experience, and thereafter documenting and disseminating this knowledge for the benefit of the wider organisation.

References

APM (2019). *APM Body of Knowledge* (7th ed.), Princes Risborough: Association for Project Management.

Kloppenborg, T. (2009). *Project Management: A Contemporary Approach*, London: Cengage Learning.

Larson, E.W. and Gray, C.F. (2018). *Project Management: The Managerial Process* (7th ed.), New York: McGraw-Hill Education.

Lock, D. (2013). *Project Management* (10th ed.), London: Gower.

Maylor, H. (2010). *Project Management* (4th ed.), London: Prentice Hall.

Murray, A. (2017). *Managing Successful Projects with PRINCE2* (6th ed.), London: The Stationary Office.

Index